hamlyn
QuickCook

D0293426

hamlyn
QuickCook
Midweek Meals

Recipes by Emma Jane Frost and Nichola Palmer

Every dish, three ways – you choose!
30 minutes | 20 minutes | 10 minutes

**DUDLEY
LIBRARIES**

000000713438	
Askews & Holts	20-Mar-2014
	£7.99
DU	

An Hachette UK Company
www.hachette.co.uk

First published in Great Britain in 2013 by Hamlyn,
a division of Octopus Publishing Group Ltd
Endeavour House, 189 Shaftesbury Avenue
London WC2H 8JY
www.octopusbooks.co.uk

Copyright © Octopus Publishing Group Ltd 2013

All rights reserved. No part of this work may be reproduced or utilized in any form
or by any means, electronic or mechanical, including photocopying, recording or by
any information storage and retrieval system, without the prior written permission
of the publisher.

ISBN 978-0-600-62646-6

A CIP catalogue record for this book is available from the British Library

Printed and bound in China

10 9 8 7 6 5 4 3 2 1

Both metric and imperial measurements are given for the recipes. Use one set
of measures only, not a mixture of both.

Standard level spoon measurements are used in all recipes
1 tablespoon = 15 ml
1 teaspoon = 5 ml

Ovens should be preheated to the specified temperature. If using a fan-assisted
oven, follow the manufacturer's instructions for adjusting the time
and temperature. Grills should also be preheated.

This book includes dishes made with nuts and nut derivatives. It is advisable for
those with known allergic reactions to nuts and nut derivatives and those who may
be potentially vulnerable to these allergies, such as pregnant and nursing mothers,
invalids, the elderly, babies and children, to avoid dishes made with nuts and nut oils.

It is also prudent to check the labels of prepared ingredients for the possible
inclusion of nut derivatives.

The Department of Health advises that eggs should not be consumed raw. This book
contains some dishes made with raw or lightly cooked eggs. It is prudent for more
vulnerable people such as pregnant and nursing mothers, invalids, the elderly, babies
and young children to avoid uncooked or lightly cooked dishes made with eggs.

Contents

Introduction 6

Meat 20
Recipes listed by cooking time 22

Chicken 72
Recipes listed by cooking time 74

Fish and Seafood 124
Recipes listed by cooking time 126

Vegetarian 176
Recipes listed by cooking time 178

Desserts 228
Recipes listed by cooking time 230

Index 280
Acknowledgements 288

Introduction

30 20 10 – Quick, Quicker, Quickest

This book offers a new and flexible approach to meal-planning for busy cooks and lets you choose the recipe option that best fits the time you have available. Inside you will find 360 dishes that will inspire you and motivate you to get cooking every day of the year. All the recipes take a maximum of 30 minutes to cook. Some take as little as 20 minutes and, amazingly, many take only 10 minutes. With a bit of preparation, you can easily try out one new recipe from this book each night and slowly you will build a wide and exciting portfolio of recipes to suit your needs.

How Does it Work?

Every recipe in the QuickCook series can be cooked one of three ways – a 30-minute version, a 20-minute version or a super-quick and easy 10-minute version. At the beginning of each chapter you'll find recipes listed by time. Choose a dish based on how much time you have and turn to that page.

You'll find the main recipe at the top of the page with a beautiful photograph and two time-variations below.

If you enjoy the dish, you can go back and cook the other time options. If you liked the 30-minute Apple and Peach Marzipan Slice (see pages 270–271), but only have 10 minutes to spare, then you'll find a way to cook it using cheat ingredients or clever shortcuts. Alternatively, browse through all the 360 recipes, find something that takes your eye and then cook the version that fits your time frame.

If you love the ingredients and flavours of the 10-minute Tomato and Mozzarella Sourdough Bruschetta (see pages 200–201), why not try the 20-minute Warm Tomato and Mozzarella Salad with Sourdough Croûtons, or be inspired to cook a more elaborate dish using similar ingredients, such as the 30-minute Tomato and Mozzarella Sourdough Bake.

Or, for easy inspiration, turn to the gallery on pages 12–19 to get an instant overview by themes, such as Mediterranean Flavours and Spicy Favourites.

QuickCook Online

To make life even easier, you can use the special code on each recipe page to email yourself a recipe card for printing, or email a text-only shopping list to your phone. Go to www.hamlynquickcook.com and enter the recipe code at the bottom of each page.

 MID-DESS-NIM

Midweek Meals

Life is busy. Most of us have to work, be it inside or outside the home, part time or full time, and walking into a kitchen on a weekday evening with half-empty cupboards and no idea of what you are going to cook for supper is a dispiriting and stressful way to end the day. Having to defrost chicken breasts or pop out for some stock cubes in order to begin a recipe can take the enjoyment out of what may otherwise have been quite a therapeutic, enjoyable activity.

For many, cooking in the week is a bore; it is a 'must-do' activity rather than a 'like-to' activity. Energy and creativity levels are low, there's very little time and there are other things you need to be getting on with. So we have come up with this book to put the pleasure back into cooking meals midweek. We believe that no matter how little time you have, cooking should be a creative, therapeutic and enjoyable process with an end result you can be proud of. But we are realistic; we know time is tight – there is paperwork to do after dinner and the house needs cleaning before your guests arrive tomorrow. So we've come up with a whole array of inspiring meals – 360 in total – to tantalize your taste buds and kick-start your creativity, and, what's more, every single one of them can be prepared and cooked in half an hour or less!

Like the other books in Hamlyn's QuickCook series, this book provides you with 120 recipes, each of which can be prepared in 30, 20 or even just 10 minutes. And because the time that you have available to cook varies each day, and because we cooks can get bored easily with a limited recipe repertoire, we have included two variations for each recipe, both of which are super-fast and taste fantastic.

Plan Healthy Balanced Meals

Some 'food in a hurry'-style cookery books assume you have an army of helpers in your kitchen and an array of special gadgets and equipment to speed up the prep process. We make no such assumptions. We do suggest, however, that you will take a little time to plan and buy for your dishes, because the key to midweek meal success is preparation. Use some of your lunch-hour or some time at the weekend to browse through this book and choose four or five meals that you'd like to serve in the week. Then, once you've worked out what ingredients you need, ensure you get everything in stock ready for the beginning of the week. Don't forget internet shopping and home-delivery services – they are designed for busy people and can be arranged for times that suit you and your busy schedule.

Mix It Up

It may seem obvious, but when you are planning your week's meals, try to get a good balance of different foods on your plate each day and through the week. We have planned the recipes in this book to help give you a broad range of nutrient-dense foods across the week, but the key is to mix up your menus and not always cook the same types of food. We would suggest that you bear the following in mind when you are creating your meal plan:

- Eat fish at least twice a week as it is known to reduce heart disease, is rich in B and D vitamins and contains high levels of Omega 3, which is great for your heart.
- Chicken can be eaten as often as your budget allows, but try to buy organic where possible.
- If you are a red meat addict, choose lean cuts where possible and cuts that lend themselves to quick cooking. Limit red meat to twice a week.
- Offal is an excellent source of vitamins, copper, iron and zinc; however, as the liver tends to accumulate chemical residues from the animal, limit your intake to once a week.
- Nuts and seeds are nutritional gems. They are low in saturated fats, high in protein and fibre and are brimming with B vitamins and many useful minerals.
- Eggs are a quick and healthy protein source and low in saturated fat – current thinking is that up to six eggs a week is a perfectly healthy addition to your diet.
- Mix up your vegetables as much as your budget allows. Include root and leafy veg and as many different colours as you can. All vegetables contain high levels of vitamin C, many contain important B vitamins and all are abundant in

fibre. What's more, when they are cooked lightly and quickly, as many are in this book, their goodness is retained and their benefits are felt all the more.

- Always choose whole grains as these are good for your heart and keep you fuller for longer.

The Storecupboard

It helps if you keep your kitchen well stocked at all times so you only have to buy the fresh and one-off ingredients each week. For those who keep their cupboards quite lean, this can be a rather time-consuming and possibly expensive exercise initially, but it is worth it to keep costs down thereafter and to reduce time spent shopping each week.

To whizz up a magical meal in minutes, you are going to need some basics in your cupboards. Plain flour and cornflour and a bottle of UHT milk for making emergency sauces, cans of chopped tomatoes, chickpeas and beans, passata, tomato paste, strong English mustard, a good selection of oils, including a basic vegetable oil such as sunflower oil, a good-quality olive oil, and some more alternative flavours, such as peanut, sesame and walnut. Always have a good-quality balsamic vinegar in the cupboard, and, for those dishes with an oriental twist, stock up on coconut milk, soy sauce, fish sauce, sweet chilli dipping sauce and hoi sin, plus a selection of your preferred noodles and rice.

Don't be afraid to buy some 'cheat' ingredients for those super-quick meals you're going to prepare: pesto sauces, ready-made pizza bases and Thai curry paste are must-haves for busy days, and don't forget you can buy garlic, ginger and lemon grass in paste form, which can be quickly and easily squeezed into the pan when cooking.

Jars of preserved vegetables are a tasty, easy addition to many pastas, salads and rice dishes, and can be stored for months (if not years) very successfully as long as they are kept cool. Therefore it would not go amiss to treat yourself to some jars of artichokes, olives and roasted red peppers, and, to add the occasional kick to your cooking, keep some capers and anchovies in stock, too; you'd be surprised how much these tiny additions give to a meal.

You may not think of yourself as a gardener, but learning to keep a few potted herbs on the windowsill will benefit you no end when it comes to adding quick and easy flavour to a midweek meal. Easy-to-keep herbs include basil, coriander, chives and rosemary. Oregano and thyme can be a little trickier to keep; however, these can be bought fresh in bunches and frozen for when you need them. Don't be concerned if the leaves go very dark or black – they will retain their flavour.

The Refrigerator and Freezer

Make space in your refrigerator for some key ingredients that form the basis for many meals: onions, garlic, hard cheese such as Cheddar and a good strong Parmesan, a carton of crème fraîche and some natural yogurt. Keep quartered lemons and limes, ginger and chillies in the freezer, plus nutrient-rich vegetables that freeze well, such as spinach, peas or sweetcorn. Bacon, chicken and fish fillets and sausages can be separated and frozen in small servings ready for easy defrosting; or buy bags of frozen prawns, mussels or mixed seafood for an easy addition to soups, stews and stir-fries.

Remember, too, that bread freezes well; bags of muffins and burger buns kept in the freezer are sure to get good use; try the delicious cod burgers on page 170 or the irresistible Eggs Benedict on page 32 for some nutritious, fast, comfort food for all the family. When a loaf of bread is no longer fresh enough to eat in slices, whizz up the loaf in a food processor and freeze the breadcrumbs in small food bags ready for coating chicken or fish fillets. For an alternative way of using your breadcrumbs, try our Cheesy Courgette Bakes on page 188 – a sure-fire winner with the vegetarians in your family.

One Pot

Everyone will love these tasty one-pot wonders.

Easy Cassoulet 24

Creamy Pork, Apple and Mustard Pan-Fry 54

Chorizo and Ham Eggs 70

Chicken and Sweetcorn Chowder 86.

Thyme-Roasted Chicken and Carrots 102

Creamy Chicken, Gammon and Leek Pan-Fry 122

Crispy Pesto Baked Cod 130

Pan-Fried Herby Salmon with Creamy Mascarpone Sauce 156

Pea, Leek and Potato Soup with Pesto and Cheesy Toasts 182

Pan-Fried Toffee Apples 242

Spiced Pan-Fried Pineapple with Rum 252

Pan-Fried Marsala Fruit and Almonds 276

Last-Minute Entertaining

Inspiring and indulgent meals for special occasions.

Balsamic Lamb Steaks with Parsnip and Potato Mash 26

Fillet Steaks with Easy Braised Red Cabbage and Blackberries 68

Chicken and Dolcelatte Pasta Bake 78

Mussels with Cider and Garlic Sauce 128

Seafood Tagliatelle 146

Asparagus, Lemon and Herb-Stuffed Salmon 148

Scallop, Bacon and Pine Nut Pan-Fry 168

Asparagus, Aubergine, Brie and Tomato Quiche 204

Goats' Cheese and Butternut Squash Stuffed Peppers 212

Berry and White Chocolate Tarts 246

Tropical Fruit and Coconut Cheesecakes 258

Baked Chocolate Orange Mousse 278

Mediterranean Flavours

Great meals that are packed with the fresh flavours of the Mediterranean.

Lamb Meatballs with Herby Feta Couscous 30

Pepperoni, Artichoke and Olive Pizzas 34

Prosciutto and Asparagus Tart 42

Risotto-Topped Lamb and Vegetable Pie 66

Chicken Parmigiana 80

Greek Chicken Stifado 100

Salt, Pepper and Chilli Squid with Chips and Garlic Mayo 134

Spinach and Feta Filo Parcels 180

Mediterranean Tomato Soup 198

Tomato and Mozzarella Sourdough Bruschetta 200

Speedy Iced Tiramisu 234

Grilled Fruit Parcels with Pistachio Yogurt 254

Spicy Favourites

Turn up the heat with this selection of hot and spicy recipes.

Moroccan Lamb Kebabs with Warm Chickpea Salad 50

Spiced Beef and Onion Chapattis 52

Paprika Chicken Quesadillas 88

Caribbean Chicken with Rice and Peas 92

Oriental Chicken Satay Stir-Fry 114

Spicy Chicken and Plantain with Caribbean Sauce 116

Chicken Jalfrezi 118

Thai Crab Cakes with Carrot Noodle Salad 144

Prawn Jambalaya 150

Chilli Seafood Stew 162

Curried Cauliflower, Lentil and Rice Pot 184

Spiced Butternut Squash Soup 194

Low-Fat Meals

Healthy recipes that don't compromise on taste.

Thai Chicken and Veg Kebab
Wraps 84

Mexican Chicken Burgers with
Tomato Salad 94

Lemon and Parsley Chicken
Skewers 96

Tuna and Bean Pasta
Salad 132

Ginger and Lime Mackerel with
Roasted Veg 136

Teriyaki Salmon with Egg
Noodles 142

Thai Green Fish Curry with
Lime Leaves 160

Oriental Prawn and Crab
Stir-Fry 172

Roasted Carrot and Beetroot
Pearl Barley with Feta 222

Baked Honeyed Figs and
Raspberries 232

Roasted Plum and Orange
Compote with Granola 236

Soft Raspberry
Meringues 260

Midweek Energy Boosters

Give your energy levels a boost with these nutrient-packed dishes.

Warm Prosciutto, Chicken Liver and Walnut Salad 58

Pan-Fried Liver with Caper Sauce and Root Mash 60

Sticky Soy Chicken with Fruity Oriental Salad 90

Warm Chicken, Med Veg and Bulgar Wheat Salad 108

Chicken, Potato and Spinach Pan-Fry 110

Smoked Fish and Fennel Pie 152

Chilli and Lemon Fishcakes 164

Falafels with Beetroot Salad and Mint Yogurt 186

Cheesy Courgette Bakes 188

Stuffed Pasta, Pine Nut and Butternut Grain 192

Chickpea, Artichoke and Tomato Pan-fry 202

Pea, Parmesan and Mint Risotto 210

Feed the Family

Great-tasting recipes that everyone will enjoy.

Spicy Sausage and Rocket Pasta 28

Garlicky Pork with Warm Butter Bean Salad 36

Lamb and Chorizo Burgers with Roasted New Potatoes 40

Spicy Sausage, Rosemary and Bean Hot Pot 62

Beef, Pumpkin and Prune Stew 64

Creamy Chicken and Tarragon Pasta 98

Honeyed Chicken and Roasted Rosemary Roots 120

Baked Herby Cod with Gruyère and Spinach Mash 158

Red Lentil Dahl with Warm Naan 216

Blueberry and Banana French Toast 250

Chocolate Tiffin Squares 256

Pan-Fried Peach and Plum Cinnamon Crunch 268

Just for Two

Special meals for just the two of you.

Eggs Benedict 32

Creamy Peppered Steaks with Sweet Potato Chips 38

Sausages in Red Wine with Creamy Layered Potatoes 56

Chicken, Pancetta and Mushroom Carbonara 106

Roasted Chicken and Spiced Butternut Squash 112

Roasted Garlicky Herb Sea Bass, Fennel and Potatoes 166

Juicy Cod Burgers with Tartare Sauce 170

Pan-Fried Proscuitto-Wrapped Salmon 174

Garlic and Herb Mushroom Tart 196

Chocolate Melting Middle Puddings 244

Apple and Peach Marzipan Slice 270

Pan-Fried Banana and Maple Syrup Brioche Rolls 274

QuickCook

Meat

Recipes listed by cooking time

30

Easy Cassoulet 24

Balsamic Lamb with Rosemary Roasties 26

Spicy Sausage Pasta Bake 28

Moroccan Lamb Meatballs with Herby Couscous 30

Poached Eggs on Ham Rosti Cakes 32

Pepperoni, Artichoke and Olive Pizzas 34

Garlicky Pork and Butter Bean Stew 36

Creamy Peppered Steaks with Sweet Potato Chips 38

Lamb and Chorizo Burgers with Roasted New Potatoes 40

Prosciutto and Asparagus Tart 42

Roast Lamb with Beans and Tomatoes 44

Tex-Mex Pork Ribs with Sweetcorn and Red Pepper Salsa 46

Bacon, Pine Nut and Parsnip Gratin 48

Moroccan Lamb Kebabs with Warm Chickpea Salad 50

Spiced Beef and Onion Curry 52

Pork, Apple and Mustard Gratins 54

Sausages in Red Wine with Creamy Layered Potatoes 56

Prosciutto, Chicken Liver and Walnut Ragù 58

Pan-Fried Liver with Caper Sauce and Root Mash 60

Spicy Sausage, Rosemary and Bean Hot Pot 62

Beef, Pumpkin and Prune Stew 64

Risotto-Topped Lamb and Vegetable Pie 66

Beef, Blackberry and Red Cabbage Stew 68

Baked Eggs with Chorizo and Ham 70

20

Chunky Sausage and Bean Soup 24

Balsamic Lamb Steaks with Parsnip and Potato Mash 26

Spicy Sausage and Rocket Pasta 28

Lamb Meatballs with Herby Feta Couscous 30

Eggs Benedict with Homemade Hollandaise Sauce 32

Pepperoni, Artichoke and Olive Tart 34

Garlicky Pork with Warm Butter Bean Salad 36

Peppered Steak Stroganoff 38

Chorizo-Topped Lamb with Spicy Chips 40

Prosciutto and Asparagus Pizza 42

Griddled Lamb Cutlets and Tomatoes with Bean Mash 44

Red Pepper Pork with Creamed Corn 46

Caramelized Bacon and Pine Nut Parsnips 48

10

One-Pan Harissa Lamb
and Chickpeas 50

Spicy Beef Rolls
with Onions 52

Creamy Pork, Apple
and Mustard Pan-Fry 54

Sausages in Red Wine Gravy
with Cheesy Potatoes 56

Chicken Livers in Prosciutto
with Walnut Salad 58

Pan-Fried Liver and Capers
with Sautéed Parsnips 60

Spicy Sausage, Rosemary
and Bean Pan-Fry 62

Beef, Pumpkin and
Prune Soup 64

Lamb and Vegetable
Risotto 66

Fillet Steaks with Easy
Braised Red Cabbage
and Blackberries 68

Chorizo and Ham Tortilla 70

Smoky Sausage and
Beans on Toast 24

Stir-Fried Balsamic Lamb
with Couscous 26

Spicy Sausage and
Rocket Baguettes 28

Lamb Burgers with Herb
and Feta Couscous 30

Eggs Benedict 32

Pepperoni, Artichoke
and Olive Crostini 34

Pork with Garlicky
Butter Bean Mash 36

Peppered Steak Wraps 38

Quick Lamb Burgers
with Chorizo 40

Crispy Prosciutto
and Chargrilled
Asparagus Salad 42

Lamb, Tomato and
Bean Pan-Fry 44

Pork, Sweetcorn and
Red Pepper Stir-Fry 46

Bacon, Pine Nut and
Parsnip Rosti 48

Harissa Lamb Pittas
with Hummus 50

Spiced Beef and
Onion Chapattis 52

Simple Pork, Apple and
Mustard Pan-Fry 54

Sausage Ball and
Red Wine Pan-Fry 56

Warm Prosciutto, Chicken
Liver and Walnut Salad 58

Quick Liver and Capers 60

Spicy Sausage and
Rosemary Sandwiches 62

Speedy Beef, Tomato
and Prune Pan-Fry 64

Lamb and Vegetable Pilaf 66

Steaks with Blackberry
Sauce and Red Cabbage 68

Chorizo and Ham Eggs 70

30 Easy Cassoulet

Serves 4

2 tablespoons olive oil

4 Cumberland sausages

4 boneless, skinless chicken
thighs, opened out flat

1 large onion, chopped

2 celery sticks, chopped

2 teaspoons smoked paprika

2 x 400 g (13 oz) cans chopped
tomatoes with garlic and herbs

2 x 400 g (13 oz) cans cannellini
beans, rinsed and drained

8 tablespoons fresh white
breadcrumbs

2 tablespoons chopped parsley

salt and pepper

- Heat 2 tablespoons of the oil in a large saucepan, add the sausages and chicken thighs and fry for 5 minutes, turning occasionally, until browned. Remove the meat from the pan and slice the sausages.

- Add the onion and celery to the pan and fry for 2–3 minutes until slightly softened. Add the paprika, stir well and return the sausages and chicken to the pan. Add the tomatoes and beans and season. Bring to the boil, then reduce the heat, cover and simmer for 20 minutes.

- Meanwhile, heat the remaining oil in a frying pan, add the breadcrumbs and fry, stirring, until golden. Serve the cassoulet sprinkled with the breadcrumbs and parsley.

---

1 Smoky Sausage and Beans on Toast

Heat 2 tablespoons olive oil in a large saucepan, add 2 chopped onions and fry for 5 minutes until softened. Add 2 x 400 g (13 oz) cans baked beans, 2 tablespoons barbecue sauce and 2 teaspoons Dijon mustard, then stir in 250 g (8 oz) sliced smoked pork sausage and heat through. Serve on thick slices of buttered wholemeal toast.

2 Chunky Sausage and Bean Soup

Heat 2 tablespoons olive oil in a large saucepan, add 2 chopped onions and 2 chopped celery sticks and fry for 5 minutes until softened. Add 2 teaspoons smoked paprika, 2 x 400 g (13 oz) cans chopped tomatoes and 2 x 400 g (13 oz) cans baked beans and bring to the boil, then reduce the heat and simmer for 10 minutes. Slice 250 g (8 oz) smoked pork sausage and stir into the soup. Heat through for 2 minutes, then serve with garlic bread.

Balsamic Lamb Steaks with Parsnip and Potato Mash

Serves 2

1 parsnip, peeled and cut into chunks

400 g (13 oz) potatoes, peeled and cut into chunks

1 tablespoon olive oil

1 onion, cut into 6 wedges

2 lean lamb leg steaks, about 150 g (5 oz) each

100 ml (3½ fl oz) red wine

1 teaspoon Dijon mustard

2 tablespoons balsamic vinegar

1 rosemary sprig, leaves stripped and chopped, plus 2 small sprigs to garnish

2–3 tablespoons crème fraîche

salt and pepper

- Cook the parsnip and potatoes in a large saucepan of lightly salted boiling water for 15 minutes until tender.

- Meanwhile, heat the oil in a large frying pan, add the onion and cook for 2–3 minutes until starting to soften. Season the lamb and add to the pan. Cook over a high heat for 5 minutes, turning once, until browned and cooked to your liking. Remove from the pan and keep warm.

- Add the wine, mustard, vinegar and chopped rosemary to the pan, bring to the boil and simmer for a few minutes until slightly thickened. Return the lamb to the pan and heat through, spooning over the sauce.

- Drain the vegetables, then return to the pan and mash with the crème fraîche and plenty of pepper. Serve the lamb and sauce on the mash, garnished with the rosemary.

 Stir-Fried Balsamic Lamb with Couscous

Place 125 g (4 oz) couscous in a heatproof bowl and cover with boiling water. Cover with clingfilm and leave to stand for 5 minutes. Meanwhile, heat 1 tablespoon vegetable oil in a wok, add 300 g (10 oz) lamb leg steaks, cut into strips, and stir-fry for 2 minutes until browned. Add ½ teaspoon garlic purée, 4 tablespoons red wine, 1 teaspoon Dijon mustard and 1 tablespoon balsamic vinegar and heat through, stirring, until bubbling. Fluff up the couscous with a fork, season and stir in a little olive oil. Serve with the lamb and rocket leaves.

 Balsamic Lamb with Rosemary

Roasties Peel 1 parsnip and 400 g (13 oz) potatoes, then cut into 1 cm (½ inch) pieces and place in a bowl. Toss with 2 tablespoons olive oil and 1 teaspoon chopped rosemary leaves and season. Tip into a roasting tin and roast in a preheated oven, 220°C (425°F), Gas Mark 7, for 25 minutes, turning occasionally, until golden and tender. Meanwhile, heat 1 tablespoon olive oil in a frying pan, add 2 seasoned lamb leg steaks, about 150 g (5 oz) each, and cook for about 5 minutes, turning once, until browned and cooked to your liking. Remove the lamb from the pan. Add 100 ml (3½ fl oz) red wine, 1 teaspoon Dijon mustard and 2 tablespoons balsamic vinegar to the pan and simmer until slightly thickened, then return the lamb and heat through in the sauce. Serve with the rosemary roasties.

 # Spicy Sausage and Rocket Pasta

Serves 4

250 g (8 oz) penne or other pasta
2 tablespoons olive oil
8 Italian-style sausages, skins
  removed
400 ml (14 fl oz) passata
1 teaspoon dried chilli flakes
4 handfuls of rocket leaves
salt and pepper
grated Parmesan cheese,
  to serve

- Cook the penne in a large saucepan of lightly salted boiling water for about 10 minutes, or until just tender.

- Meanwhile, heat the oil in a large frying pan, break the sausages into small pieces and add to the pan, then fry for 3–4 minutes, turning occasionally, until browned.

- Add the passata and chilli flakes and season. Bring to the boil, then reduce the heat and simmer for 5 minutes until the sauce is slightly reduced and the sausagemeat is cooked through.

- Drain the pasta, then add to the sauce and toss well to coat. Remove from the heat, stir in the rocket and serve with grated Parmesan.

 ### Spicy Sausage and Rocket

Baguettes Heat 2 tablespoons olive oil in a large frying pan, add 8 Italian-style sausages and fry for 8 minutes until golden and cooked through. Split 4 small baguettes and spread each with 1 teaspoon basil pesto. Add the sausages, a handful of rocket leaves and ready-made tomato salsa.

 ### Spicy Sausage Pasta Bake

Cook 250 g (8 oz) pasta in a large saucepan of lightly salted boiling water for about 10 minutes, or until just tender. Meanwhile, remove the skins of 8 Italian-style sausages and break into pieces with your fingers. Heat 2 tablespoons olive oil in a large frying pan, add the sausage pieces and fry for 3–4 minutes until golden. Add 400 ml (14 fl oz) passata and 1 teaspoon dried chilli flakes and season. Bring to the boil, then reduce the heat and simmer for 5 minutes. Drain the pasta, then add to the sauce and toss well to coat. Tip the mixture into a large ovenproof dish, then top with 250 g (8 oz) sliced mozzarella cheese. Place in a preheated oven, 200°C (400°F), Gas Mark 6, for 10 minutes until golden and bubbling. Serve with a rocket salad.

20 Lamb Meatballs with Herby Feta Couscous

Serves 2

200 g (7 oz) minced lean lamb
1 garlic clove, crushed
½ teaspoon ground cumin
½ teaspoon ground coriander
2 tablespoons olive oil
salt and pepper
raita or tzatziki, to serve

For the couscous

125 g (4 oz) couscous
1 tablespoon chopped parsley
1 tablespoon chopped mint leaves
50 g (2 oz) feta cheese, crumbled
75 g (3 oz) shop-bought
ready-cooked fresh beetroot,
chopped

- Place the lamb in a bowl, add the garlic, cumin and coriander and season. Mix well, then, using your hands, shape into 8 meatballs, pressing the mixture together firmly.

- Heat the oil in a frying pan, add the meatballs and fry over a medium heat for 8–10 minutes, or until browned and cooked through.

- Meanwhile, place the couscous in a heatproof bowl and just cover with boiling water. Cover with clingfilm and leave to stand for 5 minutes. Fluff up the couscous with a fork, then season and stir in the herbs. Lightly stir through the feta and beetroot.

- Serve the meatballs with the couscous and generous spoonfuls of raita or tzatziki.

 Lamb Burgers with Herb and Feta Couscous Soak a 100 g (3½ oz) pack coriander and lemon couscous in boiling water according to the packet instructions. Meanwhile, grill or fry 2 ready-made lamb burgers, about 125 g (4 oz) each, for about 5–8 minutes, or until cooked through, turning once. Fluff up the couscous with a fork. Stir in 50 g (2 oz) crumbled feta cheese and 75 g (3 oz) shop-bought ready-cooked fresh beetroot, chopped. Serve with the burgers.

Moroccan Lamb Meatballs with Herby Couscous Place 200 g (7 oz) minced lean lamb in a bowl, add 1 crushed garlic clove and 1 teaspoon ras el hanout (Moroccan spice blend) and season. Mix well and shape into 8 meatballs, pressing the mixture together firmly. Heat 1 tablespoon olive oil in a frying pan, add the meatballs and fry for 8–10 minutes until golden. Add a 400 g (13 oz) can chopped tomatoes and bring to the boil, then reduce the heat and simmer for 10 minutes. Meanwhile, place 125 g (4 oz) couscous in a heatproof bowl and just cover with boiling water. Cover with clingfilm and leave to stand for 5 minutes. To make the raita, stir 1 tablespoon chopped mint leaves and 2 tablespoons coarsely grated cucumber into 4 tablespoons natural yogurt. Season with pepper and set aside. Fluff up the couscous with a fork, then season and stir in 1 tablespoon each of chopped parsley and mint leaves. Serve the meatballs with the couscous and raita.

10 Eggs Benedict

Serves 2

2 large eggs
2 English muffins
6 tablespoons ready-made
  Hollandaise sauce
2 thick slices of ham
salt and pepper
chopped chives, to garnish
  (optional)

- Break the eggs into a saucepan of simmering water and cook for 3–4 minutes for a soft yolk or longer if you prefer your eggs completely set.

- Meanwhile, cut the muffins in half and toast them in a toaster or under a preheated grill. Gently warm the Hollandaise sauce in a microwaveable bowl in a microwave or in a heatproof bowl set over a saucepan of simmering water.

- Place the ham on one half of each muffin. Drain the eggs with a slotted spoon and place on the ham. Season, then spoon over the warmed Hollandaise and sprinkle with chives, if using. Top with the remaining muffin halves and serve.

 Eggs Benedict with Homemade Hollandaise Sauce To make the sauce, whisk together 2 egg yolks, 1 teaspoon white wine vinegar and 1 teaspoon lemon juice in a bowl. Gradually add 75 g (3 oz) melted butter, whisking continuously. Season and add extra lemon juice to taste. Make the Eggs Benedict as above. Spoon over the warmed Hollandaise sauce and sprinkle with chives.

 Poached Eggs on Ham Rosti Cakes Par-boil 250 g (8 oz) potatoes, peeled and halved, in a saucepan of lightly salted boiling water for 8–10 minutes. Drain and leave to cool slightly, then coarsely grate into a bowl. Add 2 slices of finely chopped ham and 2 chopped spring onions. Season and mix lightly, then shape the mixture into 2 rosti cakes. Heat 2 tablespoons olive oil in a frying pan, add the cakes and fry over a medium heat for 8–10 minutes, turning occasionally, until crisp and golden. In a separate saucepan, break 2 large eggs into simmering water and poach for 3–4 minutes or longer if you prefer a set yolk. Remove with a slotted spoon and serve on the rosti cakes with warmed ready-made Hollandaise sauce spooned over. Sprinkle with chopped chives.

30 Pepperoni, Artichoke and Olive Pizzas

Serves 2

plain flour, for dusting
145 g (5 oz) packet pizza base mix
3 tablespoons sun-dried tomato paste
125 g (4 oz) artichoke antipasti from a jar, drained
75 g (3 oz) sliced pepperoni
25 g (1 oz) pitted black olives
125 g (4 oz) mozzarella cheese, sliced
1 tablespoon olive oil
green salad, to serve

- Dust a large baking sheet with flour. Make up the pizza base mix according to the packet instructions. Turn out the dough on to a lightly floured work surface and knead until smooth and stretchy, then cut in half and roll out 2 large circles. Place on the prepared baking sheet.

- Spread the tomato paste over the bases, then top with the artichokes, pepperoni and olives. Arrange the mozzarella on top and bake in a preheated oven, 240°C (475°F), Gas Mark 9, for 10–12 minutes, or until the bases are crisp and the topping is golden.

- Drizzle the pizzas with the oil and serve with a green salad.

1 Pepperoni, Artichoke and Olive Crostini
Cut 1 small ciabatta loaf in half horizontally and place on a baking sheet. Drizzle over 2 tablespoons garlic-infused olive oil and bake in a preheated oven, 200°C (400°F), Gas Mark 6, for 5 minutes until crisp. Mix together 3 finely chopped tomatoes and 1 small finely chopped red onion in a bowl, then spoon over the bread. Top with 125 g (4 oz) artichoke antipasti from a jar, drained, 50 g (2 oz) chopped pepperoni and 8 pitted black olives. Serve with a crisp green salad.

2 Pepperoni, Artichoke and Olive Tart

Place ½ x 375 g (12 oz) sheet of ready-rolled puff pastry on a baking sheet. Spread 2 tablespoons chilli pesto over the pastry, leaving a 1 cm (½ inch) border around the edge. Top with 75 g (3 oz) artichoke antipasti from a jar, drained, 50 g (2 oz) thinly sliced pepperoni and 8 pitted black olives. Bake in a preheated oven, 200°C (400°F), Gas Mark 6, for 15 minutes, or until the pastry is crisp and golden. Serve with a rocket and Parmesan salad.

Garlicky Pork with Warm Butter Bean Salad

Serves 4

4 tablespoons olive oil
2 garlic cloves, crushed
4 lean pork chops or steaks,
   about 150 g (5 oz) each
salt and pepper

For the salad

2 tablespoons olive oil
2 x 400 g (13 oz) cans butter
   beans, rinsed and drained
12 cherry tomatoes, halved
150 ml (¼ pint) chicken stock
juice of 2 lemons
2 handfuls of parsley, chopped

• For the pork, mix together the oil and garlic in a bowl, then season. Place the pork on a foil-lined grill rack and spoon over the garlicky oil. Cook under a preheated medium grill for about 10 minutes, turning occasionally, until golden and cooked through.

• Meanwhile, make the salad. Heat the oil in a large frying pan, add the butter beans and tomatoes and heat through for a few minutes. Add the chicken stock, lemon juice and parsley and season. Serve with the grilled chops.

Pork with Garlicky Butter Bean Mash

Heat 2 tablespoons olive oil in a frying pan, add 4 seasoned thin-cut pork escalopes, about 150 g (5 oz) each, and fry for 5–6 minutes, turning occasionally, until cooked through and golden. Halfway through the cooking time add 12 halved cherry tomatoes to the pan and cook until softened, then stir in 2 handfuls of chopped parsley. Meanwhile, place 2 x 400 g (13 oz) cans butter beans, rinsed and drained, 4 tablespoons garlic-infused olive oil, salt and pepper and a little water in a blender or food processor and whizz to form a

smooth mash. Transfer to a microwaveable bowl and heat in a microwave on High for 2 minutes until hot. Serve the pork and pan juices with the butter bean mash.

Garlicky Pork and Butter Bean Stew

Heat 2 tablespoons olive oil in a large frying pan, add 4 lean pork shoulder or loin steaks, about 150 g (5 oz) each and cut into chunks, and 2 chopped onions and cook for a few minutes, stirring occasionally, until starting to brown. Add 2 crushed garlic cloves, 2 x 400 g (13 oz) cans butter beans, rinsed and drained, 2 x 400 g (13 oz) cans chopped tomatoes and a dash of Worcestershire sauce and bring to the boil, then reduce the heat and simmer for 20 minutes until the pork is cooked through. Season and stir in 2 handfuls of chopped parsley.

30 Creamy Peppered Steaks with Sweet Potato Chips

Serves 2

1 tablespoon black peppercorns, crushed

2 sirloin or rump steaks, about 200 g (7 oz) each

1 tablespoon olive oil

1 garlic clove, crushed

4 tablespoons crème fraîche

Tenderstem broccoli or green beans, to serve

For the chips

1 sweet potato, about 400 g (13 oz), scrubbed and cut into chips

2 tablespoons olive oil

salt and pepper

- Place the sweet potato in a bowl, toss with the oil and season, then spread over a baking sheet. Bake in a preheated oven, 200°C (400°F), Gas Mark 6, for 25 minutes, turning occasionally, until tender and golden.

- Meanwhile, spread the peppercorns over a plate and season with salt. Add the steaks and press the peppercorns firmly on to both sides.

- Heat a frying pan or griddle pan until hot, drizzle the steaks with the oil and cook for 3 minutes on each side for medium, or longer for well-done. Remove from the pan, cover and leave to rest.

- Add the garlic to the pan and cook for 1 minute, then stir in the crème fraîche. Bring to the boil, stirring, adding a little water if the sauce is too thick. Spoon over the steaks and serve with the chips and broccoli or green beans.

 Peppered Steak Wraps

Season both sides of 2 sirloin or rump steaks, about 200 g (7 oz) each, with plenty of coarsely ground black pepper and a little salt, pressing it on firmly, then cut into strips. Heat 1 tablespoon olive oil in a frying pan, add the steak and stir-fry over a high heat for about 3 minutes. Pile on to 2 warm soft tortillas with mixed salad leaves with beetroot. Top with spoonfuls of soured cream mixed with creamed horseradish to taste. Roll up the tortillas and serve.

 Peppered Steak Stroganoff

Season both sides of 2 sirloin or rump steaks, about 200 g (7 oz) each, with plenty of coarsely ground black pepper and a little salt, pressing it on firmly, then cut into strips. Cook 175 g (6 oz) tagliatelle or pappardelle in a saucepan of lightly salted boiling water for about 10 minutes, or until just tender. Meanwhile, heat 2 tablespoons olive oil in a wok or frying pan, add the steak strips and stir-fry over a high heat for about 3 minutes. Add 125 g (4 oz) sliced mushrooms and cook for 1 minute, then stir in 1 crushed garlic clove, 4 tablespoons crème fraîche, 1 teaspoon Dijon mustard and 1 teaspoon tomato purée. Bring to the boil, stirring, adding a little water if the sauce is too thick. Drain the pasta and serve with the stroganoff.

Lamb and Chorizo Burgers with Roasted New Potatoes

Serves 4

500 g (1 lb) minced lean lamb

250 g (8 oz) cooking chorizo, skin removed

1 garlic clove, crushed

2 tablespoons chopped parsley

2 tablespoons olive oil

4 slices of ciabatta bread, toasted

4 tablespoons fresh ready-made tomato salsa

For the potatoes

625 g (1 lb 4 oz) new potatoes, halved if large

2 tablespoons olive oil

2 rosemary sprigs, leaves stripped and roughly chopped

salt and pepper

- Place the potatoes in a large roasting tin and drizzle over the oil, then add the rosemary and season. Roast in a preheated oven, 200°C (400°F), Gas Mark 6, for 25 minutes until tender and golden.

- Meanwhile, place the lamb in a bowl and crumble in the chorizo. Add the garlic and parsley and mix well. Using your hands, shape into 4 large burgers, pressing the mixture together firmly.

- Heat the oil in a large frying pan or griddle pan, add the burgers and cook over a medium heat for 10 minutes, turning occasionally, until browned and cooked through.

- Place the burgers on the toasted ciabatta slices and top each with a spoonful of salsa. Serve with the roasted new potatoes.

Quick Lamb Burgers with Chorizo Cook 4 ready-made lamb burgers, about 125 g (4 oz) each, on a foil-lined grill rack under a preheated hot grill for 5–8 minutes, turning once, until cooked through. At the same time, grill 12 thin slices of chorizo until crisp. Top each burger with 3 slices of the chorizo, 2 slices of tomato and 2 slices of mozzarella cheese. Return to the grill and cook for 1 minute until the cheese starts to melt. Serve on toasted burger buns with salad leaves and ready-made tomato salsa.

Chorizo-Topped Lamb with Spicy Chips Sprinkle 2 teaspoons Cajun seasoning over 500 g (1 lb) frozen oven chips and cook in a preheated oven, 220°C (425°F), Gas Mark 7, for 15–20 minutes until crisp and golden. Meanwhile, heat a large frying pan or griddle pan until hot, add 250 g (8 oz) sliced chorizo sausage and fry for 2 minutes until crisp and golden. Remove from the pan and set aside. Add 4 seasoned lamb leg steaks, about 150 g (5 oz) each, to the chorizo fat in the pan and cook for 6–8 minutes, turning once, until browned and cooked to your liking. Remove the lamb from the pan and keep warm. Stir a dash of red wine vinegar into the pan juices with the juice of 2 lemons. Return the chorizo to the pan and simmer for 1 minute. Pour the chorizo and juices over the lamb steaks and serve with the chips and fresh tomato salsa.

30 Prosciutto and Asparagus Tart

Serves 2

125 g (4 oz) asparagus spears, trimmed

½ x 375 g (12 oz) sheet of ready-rolled puff pastry

1 tablespoon pesto sauce

50 g (2 oz) thinly sliced prosciutto

4 cherry tomatoes, halved

salt

To serve

Parmesan cheese shavings

rocket leaves

balsamic syrup

- Cook the asparagus in a saucepan of lightly salted boiling water for 2 minutes. Drain and rinse under cold water, then drain again.

- Place the pastry on a baking sheet. Spread the pesto sauce evenly over the pastry, leaving a 1 cm (½ inch) border around the edge. Arrange the asparagus on the pesto. Ruffle up the prosciutto and place on the top with the tomatoes.

- Bake in a preheated oven, 200°C (400°F), Gas Mark 6, for 15–20 minutes until the pastry is crisp and golden. Serve warm with Parmesan cheese shavings, rocket leaves and a drizzle of balsamic syrup.

10 Crispy Prosciutto and Chargrilled Asparagus Salad

Heat a griddle pan or frying pan until hot. Toss 175 g (6 oz) trimmed asparagus spears with 1 tablespoon olive oil in a bowl, then season. Add to the pan with 50 g (2 oz) ruffled slices of prosciutto and cook for 5–6 minutes until the asparagus is tender and the ham is crisp. Serve the asparagus and prosciutto with a peppery mix of salad leaves, halved cherry tomatoes, a drizzle of balsamic syrup and warm ciabatta bread.

20 Prosciutto and Asparagus Pizza

Spread 1 tablespoon pesto sauce over a shop-bought 23 cm (9 inch) pizza base. Top with 125 g (4 oz) trimmed thin asparagus spears, 50 g (2 oz) ruffled slices of prosciutto and 4 halved cherry tomatoes. Sprinkle over 25 g (1 oz) grated Parmesan cheese and bake in a preheated oven, 200°C (400°F), Gas Mark 6, for 15 minutes until crisp and golden. Serve in wedges with rocket leaves and a drizzle of balsamic syrup.

Griddled Lamb Cutlets and Tomatoes with Bean Mash

Serves 4

8 lamb cutlets

2 tablespoons olive oil

2 pinches of smoked paprika

1 garlic clove, crushed

2 teaspoons finely chopped rosemary leaves

400 g (13 oz) cherry vine tomatoes

For the mash

6 tablespoons olive oil

1 red chilli, deseeded and halved

2 tablespoons rosemary leaves

2 x 400 g (13 oz) cans cannellini beans, rinsed and drained

175 ml (6 fl oz) hot chicken stock

- Place the lamb, oil, paprika, garlic and rosemary in a large bowl and toss well. Leave to marinate.

- Meanwhile, make the mash. Heat the oil in a large frying pan, add the chilli and rosemary and cook for 2 minutes, then remove the chilli and rosemary with a slotted spoon.

- Return the pan to the heat, add the beans and cook for 1 minute, then pour in the stock and bring to the boil. Reduce the heat and simmer for 5 minutes until slightly reduced. Transfer to a food processor and whizz until almost smooth, retaining a little texture. Set aside and keep warm.

- Heat a large griddle pan until smoking, add the lamb and cook over a high heat for 4–5 minutes, turning once, until browned all over and cooked to your liking, adding the tomatoes around the edges for the final 2 minutes. Serve with the bean mash.

 Lamb, Tomato and Bean Pan-Fry Heat 4 tablespoons olive oil in a large frying pan, add 500 g (1 lb) thinly sliced lamb neck fillet and 2 thinly sliced red onions and cook over a high heat for 4 minutes until golden. Add 2 x 400 g (13 oz) cans cannellini beans, rinsed and drained, 350 g (11½ oz) halved cherry tomatoes and 2 tablespoons chopped rosemary leaves and stir-fry for 2–3 minutes until piping hot, then add 300 ml (½ pint) boiling chicken stock. Serve with crusty bread.

 Roast Lamb with Beans and Tomatoes Place 2 x 300 g (10 oz) lamb mini roasts in a large roasting tin, then rub each with 1 crushed garlic clove and scatter with 1 tablespoon chopped rosemary leaves. Roast in a preheated oven, 220°C (425°F), Gas Mark 7, for 10 minutes. Mix together 2 x 400 g (13 oz) cans cannellini beans, rinsed and drained, 300 ml (½ pint) hot chicken stock and 400 g (13 oz) halved cherry tomatoes and pour around the lamb, then return to the oven and cook for a further 15 minutes, or until the lamb roasts are cooked through but still slightly pink in the centre. Slice and serve with the beans and tomatoes.

30 Tex-Mex Pork Ribs with Sweetcorn and Red Pepper Salsa

Serves 2

3 tablespoons tomato ketchup

2 tablespoons soft brown sugar

2 tablespoons clear honey

1 tablespoon Worcestershire sauce

450 g (14½ oz) rack of mini pork ribs

For the salsa

300 g (10 oz) canned sweetcorn, drained

1 red pepper, cored, deseeded and thinly sliced

1 bunch of spring onions, finely chopped

4 tablespoons chopped parsley

2 tablespoons olive oil

pepper

- Mix together the ketchup, sugar, honey and Worcestershire sauce in a small bowl, then brush all over the ribs. Place the ribs in a large baking dish and bake in a preheated oven, 220°C (425°F), Gas Mark 7, for 25 minutes until golden and cooked through.

- Meanwhile, make the salsa. Mix together all the ingredients in a bowl and season well with pepper.

- Cut the pork into separate ribs and serve with the sweetcorn salsa.

 Pork, Sweetcorn and Red Pepper Stir-Fry Heat 1 tablespoon sesame oil in a wok, add 250 g (8 oz) thinly sliced pork fillet and 1 cored, deseeded and thinly sliced red pepper and stir-fry over a high heat for 4 minutes. Add 250 g (8 oz) frozen sweetcorn and 1 bunch of spring onions, finely chopped, and cook for 2 minutes, stirring occasionally. Meanwhile, mix together 3 tablespoons tomato ketchup, 1 tablespoon soft brown sugar and 1 tablespoon soy sauce. Pour in, toss and cook until piping hot. Serve with ready-cooked rice, if liked.

 Red Pepper Pork with Creamed Corn Make a large slit lengthways down the side of 2 pork steaks to form pockets. Heat 1 tablespoon olive oil in a frying pan, add 1 cored, deseeded and thinly sliced red pepper and cook over a high heat for 3–4 minutes, adding 4 finely sliced spring onions for the final 2 minutes. Stir in 2 tablespoons chopped parsley. Remove from the heat, then stuff the mixture into the pork pockets. Lightly brush with olive oil and season well. Cook under a preheated hot grill for 3–4 minutes on each side, or until golden and cooked through. Meanwhile, place 300 g (10 oz) canned creamed corn in a saucepan and heat gently for 2–3 minutes until hot, then stir in 3 tablespoons chopped parsley. Serve the pork with the creamed corn.

Caramelized Bacon and Pine Nut Parsnips

Serves 2

625 g (1 lb 6 oz) parsnips, scrubbed or peeled
50 g (2 oz) butter
175 g (6 oz) diced bacon
3 tablespoons caster sugar
50 g (2 oz) pine nuts
5 tablespoons chopped thyme leaves

- Cut the parsnips in half widthways, then cut the chunky tops into quarters lengthways and the slim bottom halves in half lengthways.

- Heat the butter in a large wok or frying pan, add the bacon and parsnips and cook over a medium heat for 15 minutes, turning and tossing occasionally, until the parsnips are golden and softened and the bacon is crisp.

- Add the caster sugar and pine nuts and cook for a further 2–3 minutes until lightly caramelized. Toss with the thyme and serve.

 Bacon, Pine Nut and Parsnip Rosti

Grate 350 g (11½ oz) peeled parsnips into a bowl and mix with 50 g (2 oz) shop-bought ready-cooked bacon rashers, snipped into small pieces, and 2 tablespoons chopped parsley. Squeeze the mixture together into 4 balls, then flatten into patties. Heat 50 g (2 oz) butter in a large frying pan, add the patties and cook over a high heat for 2 minutes on each side until golden. Serve hot, sprinkled with pine nuts, with salad.

 Bacon, Pine Nut and Parsnip Gratin

Heat 50 g (2 oz) butter in a large frying pan, add 625 g (1 lb 6 oz) peeled and thickly sliced parsnips and 175 g (6 oz) bacon, cut into small pieces, and cook for 15 minutes until golden. Add a 375 g (12 oz) pot fresh cheese sauce and 5 tablespoons chopped parsley and stir together. Transfer to a large, shallow gratin dish and scatter with 5 tablespoons fresh breadcrumbs and 3 tablespoons grated Parmesan cheese. Cook under a preheated grill for 5 minutes until the sauce is bubbling and the breadcrumbs are golden. Scatter with 2 tablespoons toasted pine nuts and 3 tablespoons chopped thyme leaves and serve.

Moroccan Lamb Kebabs with Warm Chickpea Salad

Serves 2

350 g (11½ oz) lamb neck fillet, cubed

2 teaspoons harissa paste

1 teaspoon ground cumin

1 teaspoon ground coriander

For the chickpea salad

2 tablespoons olive oil

1 large red onion, sliced

1 tablespoon cumin seeds

½ red chilli, deseeded and thinly sliced

400 g (13 oz) can chickpeas, rinsed and drained

4 tablespoons chopped coriander leaves

1 tablespoon water

40 g (1½ oz) rocket leaves

salt and pepper

- Place the lamb, harissa and ground spices in a bowl and toss well to coat. Thread on to 4 pre-soaked wooden skewers or metal ones and set aside.

- To make the chickpea salad, heat the oil in a large frying pan, add the onion and cook over a medium heat for 5 minutes until slightly golden and softened. Add the cumin seeds and chilli and cook for 1 minute. Add the chickpeas and cook for a further 2 minutes, then add the chopped coriander. Season well and set aside.

- Cook the kebabs under a preheated hot grill for 8–10 minutes, turning once, until golden and cooked through. Return the chickpeas to the heat, add the measurement water and then toss with the rocket.

- Spoon the chickpeas on to 2 warm serving plates and top with the lamb kebabs. Serve hot.

---

1 **Harissa Lamb Pittas with Hummus**

Heat 1 tablespoon olive oil in a frying pan, add 250 g (8 oz) thinly sliced lamb neck fillet and cook over a high heat for 2–3 minutes. Add 1 tablespoon harissa paste and cook, stirring, for 1 minute. Remove from the heat and stir in 2 tablespoons chopped parsley. Fill 2 pitta breads with salad leaves and top with the lamb, then spoon over shop-bought hummus and scatter with 6 halved cherry tomatoes. Serve hot.

2 **One-Pan Harissa Lamb and Chickpeas** Heat 1 tablespoon olive oil in a large wok or frying pan, add 375 g (12 oz) cubed lamb neck fillet and 1 chopped onion and cook over a high heat for 3–4 minutes until browned. Add 2 tablespoons harissa paste and a 400 g (13 oz) can chopped tomatoes. Bring to the boil, then add a 400 g (13 oz) can chickpeas, rinsed and drained. Cook for a further 3–4 minutes until the sauce is slightly reduced, then stir in 4 tablespoons

chopped coriander leaves. Serve hot with warm crusty bread.

10 Spiced Beef and Onion Chapattis

Serves 2

300 g (10 oz) thin-cut beef frying
steak, thinly sliced

1 small onion, thinly sliced

1 teaspoon ground cumin

½ teaspoon ground paprika

½ teaspoon ground coriander

2 tablespoons olive oil

1 red onion, cut into slim wedges

2 soft brown chapattis

2 tablespoons lime pickle

2 handfuls of salad leaves

salt and pepper

- Place the beef, sliced onion, spices and 1 tablespoon of the oil in a bowl and toss well to coat, then season.

- Heat the remaining oil in a frying pan, add the red onion wedges and cook over a medium heat for 2–3 minutes until softened. Add the beef and sliced onion and cook for 1–2 minutes on each side until golden and cooked through.

- Warm the chapattis according to the packet instructions. Spoon the beef and onions on to one side of each and top with the lime pickle and salad leaves, then fold over to enclose the filling and serve.

 Spicy Beef Rolls with Onions

Place 2 thin-cut beef frying steaks, about 150 g (5 oz) each, between 2 sheets of lightly oiled clingfilm and bash with a rolling pin until almost twice the size and half the thickness. Remove the clingfilm and lightly spread each steak with 1 tablespoon lime pickle and season well. Scatter each with 1 tablespoon chopped coriander leaves, then roll up tightly and secure with cocktail sticks. Heat 1 tablespoon olive oil in a frying pan, add the steak rolls and 1 thinly sliced onion and cook for 5 minutes, stirring and turning frequently, until golden. Serve scattered with extra chopped coriander.

 Spiced Beef and Onion Curry

Heat 2 tablespoons olive oil in a large frying pan, add 300 g (10 oz) cubed beef frying steak and 1 large chopped onion and cook over a high heat for 5 minutes. Add 1 tablespoon ground cumin, 1 tablespoon ground coriander and 2 teaspoons mild chilli powder and cook for 1 minute. Add a 400 g (13 oz) can chopped tomatoes and 300 ml (½ pint) hot beef stock and bring to the boil, then reduce the heat, cover and simmer over a low heat for 15 minutes. Blend 1 tablespoon cornflour with 2 tablespoons water, then add to the pan and stir until thickened. Stir in 4 tablespoons chopped coriander leaves, then serve with warm chapattis and lime pickle.

20 Creamy Pork, Apple and Mustard Pan-Fry

Serves 4

2 tablespoons olive oil

25 g (1 oz) butter

1 large red onion, cut into slim wedges

2 medium red apples, cored and cut into slim wedges

600 g (1 lb 5 oz) pork fillet, thinly sliced

300 ml (½ pint) hot chicken stock

200 ml (7 fl oz) crème fraîche

2 tablespoons Dijon mustard

2 tablespoons wholegrain mustard

6 tablespoons chopped parsley

mashed potatoes or crusty bread, to serve (optional)

- Heat the oil and butter in a large frying pan, add the onion and apples and cook over a medium-high heat for 5 minutes, turning and stirring occasionally, until golden and starting to soften. Remove with a slotted spoon and keep warm.

- Add the pork to the pan and cook over a high heat for 5 minutes until golden and cooked through. Return the onion and apples to the pan with the stock and bring to the boil. Reduce the heat and simmer for 3 minutes until the stock has reduced by half, then add the crème fraîche and mustards and heat through for 2 minutes.

- Stir in the parsley, then serve hot with mashed potatoes or crusty bread, if liked.

---

10 Simple Pork, Apple and Mustard Pan-Fry Heat 2 tablespoons olive oil and 25 g (1 oz) butter in a large frying pan, add 1 large cored and roughly chopped apple and 600 g (1 lb 5 oz) thinly sliced pork fillet and cook for 5 minutes, stirring occasionally, until golden and cooked through. Stir in 200 ml (7 fl oz) crème fraîche and 2 tablespoons wholegrain mustard until well combined. Scatter with 2 tablespoons chopped parsley and serve with ready-cooked rice or mashed potatoes, if liked.

30 Pork, Apple and Mustard Gratins Heat 2 tablespoons olive oil in a large frying pan, add 2 thinly sliced red onions, 2 cored and roughly chopped red apples and 600 g (1 lb 5 oz) thinly sliced pork fillet and cook for 8–10 minutes until golden and softened. Add 300 ml (½ pint) hot chicken stock and bring to the boil, then reduce the heat and simmer for 2 minutes until reduced by half. Stir in 200 ml (7 fl oz) crème fraîche and 2 tablespoons Dijon mustard, then divide between 4 small gratin dishes. Remove the crusts from 4 slices of wholemeal bread and place in a food processor, then whizz briefly to form chunky breadcrumbs. Transfer to a bowl and mix in 8 tablespoons grated Parmesan cheese and 2 tablespoons chopped parsley. Scatter evenly over the tops of the gratin dishes, then cook under a preheated grill for 3–4 minutes until golden and bubbling. Serve with green vegetables or salad, if liked.

Sausages in Red Wine with Creamy Layered Potatoes

Serves 2

1 tablespoon olive oil

6 good-quality sausages

1 large red onion, thinly sliced

1 tablespoon juniper berries, lightly crushed

150 ml (¼ pint) red wine

300 ml (½ pint) hot beef stock

1 teaspoon cornflour

1 tablespoon water

salt and pepper

chopped parsley, to garnish

For the potatoes

375 g (12 oz) potatoes, peeled and sliced

150 ml (¼ pint) double cream

2 tablespoons grated Parmesan cheese

- Heat the oil in a frying pan, add the sausages, onion and juniper berries and cook over a medium heat for 10–12 minutes, stirring occasionally, until cooked through.

- Pour in the red wine and stock, increase the heat and bring to the boil. Season well, then reduce the heat and simmer for about 5 minutes, stirring occasionally, until reduced by about a third. Blend the cornflour with the water, then add to the pan and stir briskly until the sauce is thickened.

- Meanwhile, cook the potatoes in a saucepan of lightly salted boiling water for 8 minutes until tender, but not losing their shape. Drain, then return to the pan, toss with the cream and season well. Transfer to a shallow gratin dish and scatter with the Parmesan. Cook under a preheated medium-hot grill for about 8–10 minutes, or until bubbling. Serve with the sausages, scattered with parsley.

---

1 Sausage Ball and Red Wine Pan-Fry

Using your hands, shape 300 g (10 oz) sausagemeat into 12 balls. Heat 1 tablespoon olive oil in a large frying pan, add the balls and cook for 4 minutes, turning occasionally, until golden. Add 1 teaspoon lightly crushed juniper berries and cook for 1 minute, then stir in a 300 g (10 oz) jar red wine cooking sauce and heat through for 3 minutes. Scatter with 2 tablespoons chopped thyme leaves and serve with ready-cooked mashed potatoes, if liked.

 2 Sausages in Red Wine Gravy with Cheesy Potatoes Cook 2 baking potatoes, about 250 g (8 oz) each, in a microwave on High for 10 minutes, or until cooked. Meanwhile, heat 1 tablespoon olive oil in a frying pan, add 4 good-quality sausages and 1 thinly sliced red onion and cook over a medium heat for 10 minutes, turning the sausages occasionally, until cooked through. Add 150 ml (¼ pint) red wine and 150 ml (¼ pint) hot chicken stock and bring to the boil, then reduce the heat and simmer for 5 minutes until reduced by half. Stir in 2 tablespoons thyme leaves and season well with pepper. When the potatoes are cooked, remove from the microwave and cut in half. Mash the insides a little with a fork and season well, then drizzle 1 tablespoon double cream and scatter 1 tablespoon grated Parmesan cheese over each. Cook under a preheated grill for 3–5 minutes until golden and bubbling. Serve the cheesy potatoes with the sausages.

1 Warm Prosciutto, Chicken Liver and Walnut Salad

Serves 2

3 tablespoons olive oil

75 g (3 oz) prosciutto, torn into big pieces

375 g (12 oz) chicken livers, drained and halved

75 g (3 oz) walnut pieces

75 g (3 oz) watercress

handful of rocket leaves

3 tablespoons balsamic vinegar

crusty bread, to serve (optional)

- Heat 1 tablespoon of the oil in a large frying pan, add the prosciutto and cook over a high heat for 2 minutes until crisp and golden, turning once. Remove from the pan and place in a large, heatproof salad bowl.

- Add the chicken livers and walnuts to the pan and cook over a high heat for 3–4 minutes until golden and the chicken livers are cooked through, but still slightly pink in the centre. Add to the prosciutto and toss in the watercress and rocket.

- In a jug, whisk together the vinegar and remaining oil, then pour over the salad and toss well to lightly coat. Serve warm with crusty bread, if liked.

2 Chicken Livers in Prosciutto with Walnut Salad

Drain 375 g (12 oz) chicken livers, then tightly wrap each with ½ slice of prosciutto and secure with cocktail sticks. Place on a foil-lined grill rack and cook under a preheated hot grill for 5–7 minutes, turning once, until golden and cooked through. Meanwhile, toss 100 g (3½ oz) watercress with 2 tablespoons olive oil, 2 tablespoons balsamic vinegar and 6 tablespoons roughly chopped walnut pieces, then place on 2 serving plates. Remove the cocktail sticks and place the chicken livers in a bowl, then toss with 1 tablespoon clear honey and 1 teaspoon wholegrain mustard. Serve the salad topped with the chicken livers.

3 Prosciutto, Chicken Liver and Walnut Ragù

Place 250 g (8 oz) peeled carrot, 1 roughly chopped onion and 125 g (4 oz) roughly chopped mushrooms in a food processor and whizz until finely chopped. Heat 4 tablespoons olive oil in a frying pan, add the vegetables and cook for 4 minutes. Add 125 g (4 oz) drained and roughly chopped chicken livers and 2 finely chopped slices of prosciutto and cook, stirring, for 5 minutes until cooked through. Add 3 tablespoons roughly chopped walnuts and cook for a further 1 minute, then add 150 ml (¼ pint) red wine and bring to the boil. Reduce the heat, cover and simmer for 10 minutes until soft. Serve with pasta.

30 Pan-Fried Liver with Caper Sauce and Root Mash

Serves 2

1 tablespoon olive oil

1 small onion, sliced into rings

2 pieces of lambs' liver, about
   250 g (8 oz) each, drained and
   cut into strips

1 tablespoon plain flour

2 tablespoons capers, drained and
   roughly chopped

150 ml (¼ pint) double cream

1 teaspoon Dijon mustard

salt and pepper

For the root mash

300 g (10 oz) peeled and cubed
   potatoes

250 g (8 oz) peeled and cubed
   carrots

175 g (6 oz) peeled parsnips,
   cut into chunks

25 g (1 oz) butter

- Cook the root vegetables in a large saucepan of lightly salted boiling water for 20 minutes until tender.

- Meanwhile, heat the oil in a frying pan, add the onion and cook over a low heat for 3 minutes until softened. Remove from the pan and keep warm.

- Place the liver on a plate and lightly sprinkle with the flour, then season on each side. Add to the hot pan and cook for 3 minutes on each side until golden brown and cooked through. Remove from the pan and keep warm.

- Return the onion to the pan with the capers, cream and mustard and gently stir until hot, but not boiling.

- Drain the vegetables, return to the pan and, using a potato masher, mash well with the butter. Season well with pepper and spoon on to 2 warm serving plates. Add the liver and sauce and serve.

---

10 Quick Liver and Capers

Toss 250 g (8 oz) drained and thinly sliced lambs' liver in 1 tablespoon seasoned plain flour mixed with ½ teaspoon mustard powder. Heat 2 tablespoons olive oil in a frying pan, add 1 thinly sliced onion and cook, stirring, over a medium heat for 2 minutes, then add the liver and cook for 4–5 minutes until cooked through. Add 1 tablespoon drained capers and 150 ml (¼ pint) double cream and bring to the boil. Serve with ready-cooked mashed potatoes.

20 Pan-Fried Liver and Capers with Sautéed Parsnips

Heat 2 tablespoons olive oil and 15 g (½ oz) butter in a large frying pan, add 375 g (12 oz) peeled and thinly sliced parsnips and cook over a medium heat for 6–7 minutes until golden and cooked through. Remove with a slotted spoon and keep warm. Meanwhile, heat a further 1 tablespoon olive oil in the pan. Toss 250 g (8 oz) drained and thinly sliced lambs' liver in 1 tablespoon seasoned plain

flour and cook in the hot oil for 2 minutes, then add 1 thinly sliced red onion and cook for a further 3–4 minutes until softened and golden and the meat is cooked through. Add 1 tablespoon drained capers and 150 ml (¼ pint) double cream and toss and stir for 2 minutes until piping hot. Serve with the parsnips.

30 Spicy Sausage, Rosemary and Bean Hot Pot

Serves 4

12 good-quality pork sausages

2 tablespoons olive oil

1 large red onion, cut into slim wedges

2 tablespoons rosemary leaves

1 small mild red chilli, deseeded and thinly sliced

4 tomatoes, roughly chopped

2 x 400 g (13 oz) cans butter beans, rinsed and drained

400 g (13 oz) can flageolet beans, rinsed and drained

600 ml (1 pint) passata

warm crusty bread, to serve

- Cook the sausages under a preheated hot grill for 8–10 minutes, turning occasionally, until cooked through.

- Meanwhile, heat the oil in a large saucepan, add the onion and cook over a medium heat for 3–4 minutes until slightly softened, then add the rosemary and chilli and cook for a further 2 minutes. Add the tomatoes and cook for 3 minutes, stirring occasionally, then add the beans and passata and bring to the boil.

- Reduce the heat, add the sausages, cover and simmer for 15 minutes, stirring occasionally, until piping hot and the sauce is thick, adding a little water if necessary. Serve with warm crusty bread.

 1 **Spicy Sausage and Rosemary Sandwiches** Heat 2 tablespoons olive oil in a large frying pan, add 8 good-quality chipolata sausages, 1 large thinly sliced red onion and 2 tablespoons rosemary leaves and cook for 8–10 minutes, turning frequently, until golden and cooked through. Cut 4 small, slim French bread rolls in half. Spread the top half of each with 1 tablespoon chilli jam, then fill each with 2 sausages, onions and rosemary and top with a handful of rocket leaves.

2 **Spicy Sausage, Rosemary and Bean Pan-Fry** Cook 12 good-quality sausages under a preheated hot grill for 10 minutes until cooked through, turning occasionally. Remove from the grill and slice thickly. Meanwhile, heat 2 tablespoons olive oil in a large frying pan, add 2 thinly sliced onions and cook for 3–4 minutes, then add 2 tablespoons chopped rosemary leaves and 2 teaspoons dried chilli flakes. Add the sausages and 2 x 400 g (13 oz) cans flageolet beans, rinsed and drained, and 400 ml (14 fl oz) passata. Bring to the boil, then reduce the heat and simmer for 10 minutes. Serve with warm crusty bread.

30 Beef, Pumpkin and Prune Stew

Serves 4

2 tablespoons olive oil

1 garlic clove, chopped

1 large onion, chopped

500 g (1 lb) peeled, deseeded and cubed pumpkin

600 g (1 lb 5 oz) steak, such as sirloin, rump or frying, cubed

2 teaspoons ground coriander

2 teaspoons ground cumin

150 g (5 oz) ready-to-eat soft dried prunes

2 x 400 g (13 oz) cans chopped tomatoes

450 ml (¾ pint) hot beef stock

100 g (3½ oz) coriander leaves, chopped

To serve

couscous (optional)

natural yogurt

- Heat the oil in a large saucepan or flameproof casserole, add the garlic, onion, pumpkin and beef and cook over a high heat for 5–10 minutes until the beef is browned and the pumpkin is golden. Add the spices and cook for a further 1 minute.

- Add the prunes, tomatoes and stock and bring to the boil, then reduce the heat, cover and simmer for 15 minutes, stirring occasionally, until the stew is thickened and the meat and vegetables are cooked through.

- Scatter over the chopped coriander and stir through. Serve with couscous, if liked, topped with spoonfuls of yogurt.

 Speedy Beef, Tomato and Prune Pan-Fry Heat 2 tablespoons olive oil in a large frying pan, add 600 g (1 lb 5 oz) thinly sliced beef frying steak and cook over a high heat for 2 minutes. Add 2 teaspoons ground coriander, 2 teaspoons ground cumin and 8 chopped tomatoes and cook for a further 2–3 minutes until softened. Serve hot, scattered with 12 roughly chopped ready-to-eat dried prunes and 2 tablespoons chopped coriander leaves.

Beef, Pumpkin and Prune Soup Heat 2 tablespoons olive oil in a large saucepan, add 500 g (1 lb) peeled, deseeded and cubed pumpkin and 2 tablespoons ground coriander and cook for 5 minutes, stirring occasionally, until softened. Add 2 x 400 g (13 oz) cans chopped tomatoes and 450 ml (¾ pint) hot beef stock and bring to the boil, then reduce the heat, cover and simmer for 8 minutes until tender. Meanwhile, heat 2 tablespoons olive oil in a large frying pan, add 350 g (11½ oz) finely diced beef frying steak and cook over a high heat for 3–4 minutes until golden and cooked. Remove from the heat and set aside. Place the pumpkin mixture in a food processor and whizz until smooth. Return to the heat and add the chopped steak and 8 roughly chopped ready-to-eat dried prunes. Serve sprinkled with chopped coriander leaves.

30 Risotto-Topped Lamb and Vegetable Pie

Serves 2

175 g (6 oz) risotto rice

2 tablespoons olive oil

375 g (12 oz) courgettes, roughly chopped

1 small aubergine, roughly chopped

300 g (10 oz) minced lamb

2 tomatoes, roughly chopped

400 g (13 oz) can chopped tomatoes

1 egg

125 g (4 oz) Cheddar cheese, grated

salt and pepper

rocket salad, to serve (optional)

- Cook the rice in a saucepan of lightly salted boiling water for 20 minutes until tender.

- Meanwhile, heat the oil in a large frying pan, add the courgettes and aubergine and cook over a high heat for 5 minutes, then add the lamb and cook for a further 10 minutes until the meat is browned.

- Add the fresh tomatoes and cook, stirring, for 2 minutes, then add the canned tomatoes and bring to the boil. Reduce the heat, cover and simmer for 5 minutes.

- Drain the rice and place in a bowl, then mix in the egg and two-thirds of the cheese. Season well.

- Spoon the lamb and vegetables into a shallow gratin dish, then spoon the rice mixture over the top. Scatter with the remaining cheese. Cook under a preheated hot grill for 2–3 minutes until golden. Serve hot with a rocket salad, if liked.

 Lamb and Vegetable Pilaf

Heat 2 tablespoons olive oil in a large saucepan, add 250 g (8 oz) thinly sliced lamb neck fillet and 250 g (8 oz) halved and thinly sliced courgettes and cook over a high heat for 5 minutes until cooked through. Add 4 roughly chopped tomatoes and cook for a further 2 minutes, then add a 250 g (8 oz) pack ready-cooked rice and cook for 2 minutes until piping hot. Season well and serve.

 Lamb and Vegetable Risotto

Heat 1 tablespoon olive oil in a large frying pan, add 1 roughly chopped onion and cook for 2 minutes, then add 175 g (6 oz) risotto rice and 600 ml (1 pint) hot rich chicken stock and bring to the boil. Reduce the heat, cover and simmer over a low heat for 15 minutes, stirring occasionally, until tender. Meanwhile, heat 1 tablespoon olive oil in a separate frying pan, add 175 g (6 oz) minced lamb and 1 roughly chopped courgette and cook for 10 minutes until golden and cooked through, adding 2 roughly chopped tomatoes for the final 2–3 minutes. Once the rice is tender and cooked, stir in the lamb and vegetables. Season well and serve.

Fillet Steaks with Easy Braised Red Cabbage and Blackberries

Serves 2

2 fillet steaks, about 150 g
(5 oz) each
15 g (½ oz) butter
salt and pepper
mashed potatoes, to serve
(optional)

For the red cabbage

2 tablespoons olive oil
1 red onion, thinly sliced
½ red cabbage, thinly shredded
3 tablespoons balsamic vinegar
4 tablespoons soft brown sugar
1 teaspoon allspice
2 tablespoons redcurrant jelly
125 g (4 oz) blackberries

- To make the red cabbage, heat the oil in a saucepan, add the onion and cook over a medium heat for 3 minutes, then add the red cabbage and cook for a further 3 minutes, stirring continuously.

- Add the vinegar, sugar and allspice, cover and cook over a very low heat for 10 minutes until the cabbage is soft and tender, adding the redcurrant jelly and blackberries for the final 3 minutes.

- Meanwhile, season the steaks well. Heat the butter in a frying pan, add the steaks and cook over a high heat for 2–3 minutes on each side until browned and cooked to your liking.

- Spoon the red cabbage on to 2 warm serving plates and top with the steaks. Serve with mashed potatoes, if liked.

 Steaks with Blackberry Sauce and Red Cabbage Heat 25 g (1 oz) butter in a large frying pan, add ¼ finely shredded red cabbage, 1 teaspoon lightly crushed juniper berries and ½ teaspoon allspice and cook over a medium heat for 5 minutes. In a separate frying pan, heat 15 g (½ oz) butter and cook 2 thin 125 g (4 oz) seasoned rump or sirloin steaks to your liking, turning halfway through cooking. Add 75 g (3 oz) blackberries and 5 tablespoons redcurrant jelly and stir until melted. Serve the steaks with the red cabbage, with the sauce spooned over.

 Beef, Blackberry and Red Cabbage Stew Heat 2 tablespoons olive oil in a large saucepan, add 300 g (10 oz) cubed beef steak, such as rump, sirloin or frying, and cook for 2 minutes, then add 1 sliced red onion, 2 teaspoons lightly crushed juniper berries, 1 teaspoon ground allspice and ¼ shredded red cabbage and cook for a further 5 minutes. Add 1 raw beetroot, peeled and cut into slim wedges, and cook for 1 minute. Add 300 ml (½ pint) hot beef stock and 150 ml (¼ pint) red wine and bring to the boil. Reduce the heat, cover and simmer gently for 15 minutes, then add 125 g (4 oz) blackberries. Cook for a further 3–4 minutes until the blackberries have just lost their shape. Blend 1 teaspoon cornflour with 1 tablespoon water, then add to the pan and stir until thickened. Serve with crusty wholemeal bread to mop up the juices.

10 Chorizo and Ham Eggs

Serves 2

1 tablespoon olive oil

1 small red pepper, cored,
deseeded and sliced

125 g (4 oz) thinly sliced chorizo

2 tomatoes, roughly chopped

50 g (2 oz) wafer-thin ham

2 handfuls of baby spinach leaves

2 large eggs

warm crusty bread, to serve

- Heat the oil in a frying pan, add the red pepper and chorizo and cook over a high heat for 2 minutes until golden. Add the tomatoes and cook for a further 2 minutes, then add the ham and spinach and cook, stirring occasionally, for 2 minutes.

- Divide the mixture between 2 small, individual pans, if you have them (if not, continue to cook in one pan). Make wells in the tomato mixture and break the eggs into the wells. Cook for 2–3 minutes over a medium heat until set. Serve with warm crusty bread to mop up the juices.

20 Chorizo and Ham Tortilla

Heat 3 tablespoons olive oil in a large, flameproof frying pan, add 125 g (4 oz) thickly sliced chorizo, 1 sliced red onion and ½ cored, deseeded and thinly sliced red pepper and cook for 5 minutes until softened, then add 50 g (2 oz) wafer-thin ham, torn into small pieces. In a jug, whisk together 5 eggs with plenty of salt and pepper. Add a large handful of spinach leaves to the pan and stir for 2 minutes until wilted. Pour in the eggs and cook over a low heat until the base is set. Place the pan under a preheated hot grill and cook the tortilla for 3–4 minutes until the top is firm and set. Serve cut into wedges.

30 Baked Eggs with Chorizo and Ham

Heat 2 tablespoons olive oil in a frying pan, add 125 g (4 oz) roughly diced chorizo and ½ cored, deseeded and diced red pepper and cook for 5 minutes until golden and softened. Lightly grease 2 ramekin dishes and break 2 eggs into each. Mix 2 tablespoons chopped parsley and 25 g (1 oz) wafer-thin ham, shredded, into the chorizo mixture and scatter over the eggs, then season well. Place in a roasting tin and pour in enough boiling water to come halfway up the sides of the dishes. Bake in a preheated oven, 200°C (400°F), Gas Mark 6, for 20 minutes until firm and set. Serve with wilted spinach and crusty bread.

QuickCook
Chicken

Recipes listed by cooking time

30

Chicken and Sweet Potato
Curry   76

Chicken and Dolcelatte
Pasta Bake   78

Chicken Parmigiana   80

Roasted Lemony Chicken
with Courgettes   82

Thai Chicken with
Veg Rice   84

Creamy Chicken and
Sweetcorn Chowder   86

Smoky Chicken Quesadillas
with Sweetcorn Salsa   88

Sticky Soy Chicken with
Fruity Oriental Salad   90

Caribbean Chicken with
Rice and Peas   92

Mexican Roasted Chicken
Tortillas   94

Baked Lemon and
Parsley Chicken   96

Baked Chicken with
Creamy Tarragon Sauce   98

Greek Chicken Stifado   100

Thyme-Roasted Chicken
and Carrots   102

Chicken, Chorizo and
Lentil Soup   104

Chicken, Pancetta and
Mushroom Pasta Bake   106

Warm Chicken, Med Veg
and Bulgar Wheat Salad   108

Chicken, Spinach and
Potato Gratin   110

Roasted Chicken and Spiced
Butternut Squash   112

Satay Chicken Skewers with
Oriental Veg Stir-Fry   114

Spiced Chicken and
Plantain Stew   116

Chicken Jalfrezi   118

Honeyed Chicken
and Roasted
Rosemary Roots   120

Creamy Chicken, Gammon
and Leek Gratin   122

20

Chicken, Potato and
Pea Curry   76

Chicken and Dolcelatte
Pasta Gratin   78

Chicken in Cheesy Aubergine
and Tomato Sauce   80

Lemon Chicken and
Courgette Risotto   82

Thai Chicken and
Veg Kebab Wraps   84

Chicken and Sweetcorn
Chowder   86

Paprika Chicken
Quesadillas   88

Sticky Soy Chicken and
Pineapple Skewers   90

Caribbean Chicken,
Rice and Pea Pot   92

Mexican Chicken Burgers
with Tomato Salad   94

Lemon and Parsley-Stuffed
Chicken   96

Creamy Chicken and
Tarragon Pasta   98

Chicken, Artichoke and
Olive Pasta   100

Sticky Chicken and
Carrots with Thyme   102

10

Chicken and Chorizo Kebabs with Lentil Purée	104
Chicken, Pancetta and Mushroom Carbonara	106
Chicken and Med Veg Kebabs with Herby Bulgar Wheat	108
Chicken, Potato and Spinach Pan-Fry	110
Spiced Chicken and Butternut Soup	112
Oriental Chicken Satay Stir-Fry	114
Spicy Chicken with Plantain Chips	116
Spicy Chicken Stir-Fry	118
Rosemary and Honey-Glazed Chicken and Roots	120
Leek-Stuffed Chicken in Prosciutto	122

Chicken Saag Aloo	76
Chicken and Dolcelatte Tagliatelle	78
Cheat's Chicken Parmigiana	80
Lemon Chicken and Courgette Stir-Fry	82
Thai Chicken and Veg Noodles	84
Quick Chicken and Sweetcorn Soup	86
Chicken Tortilla Toasties	88
Spicy Chicken with Soy and Pineapple Noodles	90
Quick Caribbean Chicken	92
Fully Loaded Chicken Nachos	94
Lemon and Parsley Chicken Skewers	96
Creamy Chicken and Tarragon Pan-Fry	98
Chicken, Artichoke and Olive Pan-Fry	100
Pan-Fried Chicken, Carrots and Thyme	102

Chicken and Chorizo with Green Lentils	104
Creamy Chicken, Pancetta and Mushroom Pasta	106
Warm Chicken and Med Veg Pittas	108
Simple Chicken and Spinach with Mash	110
Spicy Chicken Strips with Sweet Potatoes	112
Quick Chicken Satay Stir-Fry	114
Spicy Chicken and Plantain with Caribbean Sauce	116
Speedy Chicken Curry	118
Simple Honeyed Rosemary Chicken and Roots	120
Creamy Chicken, Gammon and Leek Pan-Fry	122

30 Chicken and Sweet Potato Curry

Serves 4

2 tablespoons vegetable oil

1 large onion, chopped

1 medium red chilli, deseeded and chopped

500 g (1 lb) boneless, skinless chicken breasts, chopped

600 g (1 lb 5 oz) sweet potatoes, peeled and cut into chunks

2–4 tablespoons korma curry paste

400 ml (14 fl oz) can coconut milk

400 g (13 oz) can chopped tomatoes

250 g (8 oz) green beans, trimmed and halved

2 tablespoons chopped coriander leaves

boiled basmati rice, to serve

- Heat the oil in a large saucepan, add the onion and cook for 2–3 minutes until softened. Add the chilli, chicken and sweet potatoes and cook for 5 minutes, stirring occasionally.

- Add the korma paste and cook for 1 minute, then add the coconut milk, tomatoes and green beans. Bring to the boil, then reduce the heat, cover and simmer for 15 minutes until the sweet potato is tender and the chicken is cooked through.

- Stir the coriander into the boiled basmati rice and serve with the curry.

10 Chicken Saag Aloo

Heat 2 tablespoons vegetable oil in a large frying pan, add 500 g (1 lb) chicken mini-fillets and cook over a high heat for 2 minutes until golden. Add 2 tablespoons korma curry paste and 6 tablespoons water. Heat for 1 minute, then stir in 2 x 300 g (10 oz) packs fresh saag aloo. Cook for 5 minutes, stirring occasionally, until piping hot and the chicken is cooked through. Serve with garlic and coriander naan bread.

20 Chicken, Potato and Pea Curry

Heat 4 tablespoons vegetable oil in a large saucepan, add 500 g (1 lb) chicken mini-fillets and stir-fry over a high heat for 2 minutes until golden. Add 1 teaspoon garlic purée and 2–4 tablespoons korma curry paste. Cook for 1 minute, then add a 400 ml (14 fl oz) can coconut milk and a 400 g (13 oz) can chopped tomatoes. Stir in 2 x 300 g (10 oz) cans new potatoes, drained and chopped, and 250 g (8 oz) frozen peas. Bring to the boil, then reduce the heat, cover and simmer for 10 minutes until cooked through. Stir in 2 tablespoons chopped coriander leaves and serve with boiled basmati rice.

Chicken and Dolcelatte Pasta Bake

Serves 2

2 tablespoons olive oil
1 small onion, chopped
175 g (6 oz) skinless chicken breast fillets, chopped
150 ml (¼ pint) double cream
75 ml (3 fl oz) dry white wine
1 teaspoon wholegrain mustard
175 g (6 oz) pasta, such as penne
125 g (4 oz) broccoli florets
75 g (3 oz) dolcelatte cheese, chopped
25 g (1 oz) fresh breadcrumbs
salt and pepper
green salad, to serve

- Heat 1 tablespoon of the oil in a frying pan, add the onion and cook for 2 minutes, then add the chicken and cook for a further 5 minutes until cooked through. Stir in the cream, wine and mustard and simmer for 5 minutes.

- Meanwhile, cook the pasta in a saucepan of lightly salted boiling water for 10 minutes, or until just tender, adding the broccoli for the final 5 minutes. Drain, add to the sauce and stir well to coat. Add the cheese, stir well and season.

- Tip the mixture into an ovenproof dish, sprinkle over the breadcrumbs and drizzle over the remaining oil. Bake in a preheated oven, 200°C (400°F), Gas Mark 6, for 15 minutes until golden and bubbling. Serve with a green salad.

 Chicken and Dolcelatte Tagliatelle Heat 1 tablespoon olive oil in a frying pan, add 175 g (6 oz) chicken mini-fillets and fry for 2 minutes until golden. Add 150 ml (¼ pint) double cream, 75 ml (3 fl oz) dry white wine and 1 teaspoon wholegrain mustard and simmer for 5 minutes until the chicken is cooked through. Meanwhile, cook 250 g (8 oz) fresh egg tagliatelle and 75 g (3 oz) frozen peas in a saucepan of lightly salted boiling water for 3 minutes, or until just tender. Add 75 g (3 oz) chopped dolcelatte cheese to the sauce and stir until melted, then season. Drain the tagliatelle, add to the sauce and lightly stir to coat.

 Chicken and Dolcelatte Pasta Gratin Cook 175 g (6 oz) pasta, such as penne, in a large saucepan of lightly salted boiling water for 10 minutes, or until just tender, adding 125 g (4 oz) frozen broccoli florets for the final 5 minutes. Meanwhile, heat 1 tablespoon olive oil in a frying pan, add 175 g (6 oz) chicken mini-fillets and fry for 2 minutes until golden. Add 150 ml (¼ pint) double cream, 75 ml (3 fl oz) dry white wine and 1 teaspoon wholegrain mustard and simmer for 5 minutes until the chicken is cooked through. Drain the pasta and broccoli, add to the sauce and toss well to coat. Stir in 75 g (3 oz) chopped dolcelatte cheese, season and tip into a flameproof dish. Sprinkle over 2 tablespoons grated Parmesan cheese and cook under a preheated medium grill for 5 minutes until golden.

30 Chicken Parmigiana

Serves 2

4 tablespoons olive oil
1 small aubergine, sliced
1 garlic clove, crushed
300 ml (½ pint) passata
1 tablespoon chopped fresh
   oregano, plus extra to garnish
2 tablespoons plain flour
1 egg, beaten
75 g (3 oz) fresh white
   breadcrumbs
2 small skinless chicken breast
   fillets, about 150 g (5 oz) each,
   halved horizontally
125 g (4 oz) mozzarella cheese,
   sliced
salt and pepper
spaghetti, to serve

- Heat 2 tablespoons of the oil in a very large, flameproof frying pan, add the aubergine slices and fry for 1 minute on each side. Add the garlic, passata and oregano and season. Bring to the boil, then reduce the heat, cover and simmer for 10 minutes, stirring occasionally.

- Meanwhile, place the flour, beaten egg and breadcrumbs on separate plates. Dip the chicken pieces in the flour, shaking off any excess, then coat in the egg and finally the breadcrumbs, pressing them on firmly.

- Heat the remaining oil in a very large frying pan, add the coated chicken and cook for about 5 minutes on each side until golden and cooked through. Place on top of the aubergine sauce and top with the mozzarella.

- Place the pan under a preheated medium grill for 3–4 minutes until the cheese is melted. Garnish with oregano and serve with spaghetti.

---

10 Cheat's Chicken Parmigiana

Heat 2 tablespoons olive oil in a large, flameproof frying pan, add a 300 g (10 oz) pack breaded chicken mini-fillets and fry for 8 minutes, turning occasionally, until golden and cooked through. Meanwhile, heat a 325 g (11 oz) jar tomato pasta sauce in a large saucepan until hot. Pour over the chicken and top with 125 g (4 oz) sliced mozzarella cheese. Place the pan under a preheated medium grill for 2 minutes until the cheese is melted. Serve with a crisp green salad.

20 Chicken in Cheesy Aubergine and

Tomato Sauce Cut 2 small boneless, skinless chicken breasts, about 150 g (5 oz) each, in half horizontally. Heat 2 tablespoons olive oil in a very large, flameproof frying pan, add the chicken and fry for 2–3 minutes on each side until browned. Add 1 small aubergine, cut into chunks, and cook for 2 minutes until golden, adding an extra tablespoon of oil if needed. Stir in 1 crushed garlic clove, 300 ml (½ pint) passata and 1 tablespoon chopped

fresh oregano or ½ teaspoon dried oregano and season. Cover and simmer for 10 minutes until cooked through. Remove the lid and arrange 125 g (4 oz) sliced mozzarella cheese over the top. Place the pan under a preheated medium grill for 2 minutes until the cheese is melted. Serve with spaghetti.

3⏲ Roasted Lemony Chicken with Courgettes

Serves 2

4 chicken thighs, about 100 g
  (3½ oz) each
finely grated rind of 1 lemon
1 garlic clove, crushed, plus
  2 whole cloves, unpeeled
4 tablespoons olive oil
375 g (12 oz) new potatoes,
  halved if large
1 red onion, cut into wedges
1 courgette, thickly sliced
1 tablespoon thyme leaves, plus
  a few sprigs to garnish
salt and pepper

- Cut a few slashes across each chicken thigh. Mix together the lemon rind, crushed garlic and 2 tablespoons of the oil in a bowl, then rub the mixture over the chicken, pushing it into the slashes. Place in a roasting tin with the potatoes and season. Roast in a preheated oven, 220°C (425°F), Gas Mark 7, for 10 minutes.

- Add the onion, courgette, unpeeled garlic and thyme leaves to the tin and drizzle with the remaining oil. Return to the oven and roast for a further 15 minutes, or until the chicken is golden and cooked through and the vegetables are tender.

- Squeeze the soft garlic over the chicken and vegetables, discarding the skin, and serve garnished with thyme sprigs.

 Lemon Chicken and Courgette Stir-Fry

Heat 1 tablespoon vegetable oil in a wok or large frying pan, add 250 g (8 oz) chicken mini-fillets and stir-fry over a high heat for 2 minutes until golden. Add 1 chopped courgette and 4 chopped spring onions and stir-fry for a further 2 minutes until the vegetables are just tender and the chicken is cooked through. Stir in a 120 g (4 oz) sachet lemon stir-fry sauce. Heat through, then stir in the leaves from 1 head of pak choi and cook until just wilted. Serve with ready-cooked rice.

 Lemon Chicken and Courgette Risotto

Heat 1 tablespoon olive oil in a frying pan, add 175 g (6 oz) chopped skinless chicken breast fillets and 1 crushed garlic clove and fry for 2 minutes until golden. Add 1 chopped courgette and fry for a further 2 minutes, then stir in ½ x 175 g (6 oz) pack asparagus-flavoured quick-cook risotto rice. Cook for 12 minutes according to the packet instructions until the rice is creamy and the chicken is cooked through. Stir in 1 teaspoon finely grated lemon rind and season to taste. Serve sprinkled with grated Parmesan cheese.

20 Thai Chicken and Veg Kebab Wraps

Serves 4

2 tablespoons Thai red curry paste

juice of 2 limes

4 tablespoons natural yogurt, plus extra to serve

2 tablespoons coconut milk

400 g (13 oz) skinless chicken breast fillets, cut into chunks

1 red pepper, cored, deseeded and cut into chunks

1 large courgette, thickly sliced

2 tablespoons olive oil

4 large soft tortilla wraps

½ cucumber, cut into sticks

2 handfuls of bean sprouts

sweet chilli sauce, to serve

- Mix together the curry paste, lime juice, yogurt and coconut milk in a large, non-metallic bowl. Add the chicken and stir well to coat. Leave to marinate for 5 minutes.

- Thread the chicken pieces on to 8 metal skewers, alternating with the red pepper and courgette. Drizzle with the oil and cook under a preheated medium grill for 8–10 minutes, turning occasionally, until the chicken is cooked through and just starting to char and the vegetables are tender.

- Meanwhile, warm the tortillas in a microwave. Divide the cucumber and bean sprouts between the wraps, top with the grilled chicken and vegetables and add a dash of sweet chilli sauce and a spoonful of yogurt to each. Roll up the tortilla wraps and serve.

---

10 Thai Chicken and Veg Noodles

Heat 2 tablespoons vegetable oil in a wok, add 500 g (1 lb) chicken mini-fillets and stir-fry over a high heat for 2 minutes until golden. Add 4–6 teaspoons Thai red curry paste and the juice of 2 limes and stir-fry for 1 minute, then stir in 2 x 250 g (8 oz) packs ready-prepared stir-fry vegetables and cook for a further 2 minutes until the vegetables are just tender and the chicken is cooked through. Add a 300 g (10 oz) pack ready-cooked noodles and heat through, stirring, then add a dash of soy sauce and sweet chilli sauce and serve.

30 Thai Chicken with Veg Rice

Cut a few slashes across 4 boneless, skinless chicken breasts, about 150 g (5 oz) each. Mix together 2 tablespoons Thai red curry paste, the juice of 2 limes and 8 tablespoons natural yogurt in a large non-metallic dish. Add the chicken and turn to coat. Leave to marinate for 10 minutes. Heat 2 tablespoons vegetable oil in a large frying pan, add 2 crushed garlic cloves, 2 cored, deseeded and chopped red peppers and 2 chopped courgettes and fry for 2–3 minutes. Stir in 300 g (10 oz) jasmine rice and coat in the oil. Add 600 ml (1 pint) hot chicken stock and bring to the boil, then reduce the heat, cover and simmer for 10 minutes until the stock has been absorbed and the rice is tender. Stir in 2 tablespoons chopped coriander leaves. Meanwhile, cook the chicken on a foil-lined grill rack under a preheated medium grill for 10–15 minutes, turning occasionally, until cooked through and just starting to char at the edges. Serve the chicken with the rice, extra yogurt and a drizzle of sweet chilli sauce.

2 Chicken and Sweetcorn Chowder

Serves 2

25 g (1 oz) butter
150 g (5 oz) potatoes, peeled and cut into small chunks
2 spring onions, chopped
2 streaky bacon rashers, chopped
150 g (5 oz) skinless chicken breast fillet, chopped
150 ml (¼ pint) hot chicken stock
295 g (10 oz) can condensed mushroom soup
200 ml (7 fl oz) milk
75 g (3 oz) frozen or canned sweetcorn
1 tablespoon chopped parsley
salt and pepper
crusty bread, to serve

• Heat the butter in a saucepan, add the potatoes, spring onions, bacon and chicken and fry for 5 minutes, stirring. Pour in the stock and simmer for 5 minutes until the potatoes are tender and the chicken is cooked through.

• Add the soup, milk and sweetcorn and bring to the boil, stirring, then reduce the heat, cover and simmer for 5 minutes. Season and add the parsley. Serve with crusty bread.

1 Quick Chicken and Sweetcorn Soup

Heat 15 g (½ oz) butter in a saucepan, add 150 g (5 oz) chopped skinless chicken breast fillet, 2 chopped streaky bacon rashers and 2 chopped spring onions and cook for 5 minutes, stirring, until the chicken and bacon are cooked through. Add a 600 ml (1 pint) carton creamy vegetable soup and 75 g (3 oz) frozen or canned sweetcorn and heat through for 4–5 minutes until piping hot. Sprinkle with chopped parsley and serve with crusty bread.

3 Creamy Chicken and Sweetcorn

Chowder Heat 25 g (1 oz) butter in a saucepan, add 1 chopped onion, 2 chopped streaky bacon rashers, 150 g (5 oz) peeled and chopped potatoes and 1 chopped celery stick and cook for 5 minutes. Pour in 450 ml (¾ pint) hot chicken stock and add 125 g (4 oz) frozen or canned sweetcorn and 1 whole boneless, skinless chicken breast, about 150 g (5 oz). Bring to the boil, then reduce the heat, cover and simmer for 10 minutes until the vegetables are tender and the chicken is cooked through. Remove the chicken from the pan and set aside. Blend the soup with a stick blender until creamy but still with some vegetable pieces. Chop the chicken and return to the pan, then add 1 tablespoon chopped parsley and 4 tablespoons single cream. Season and heat through. Serve with garlic bread.

Paprika Chicken Quesadillas

Serves 2

1 tablespoon olive oil

1 teaspoon smoked paprika

1 garlic clove, crushed

350 g (11½ oz) chicken mini-fillets

2 soft flour tortillas, halved

125 g (4 oz) Cheddar cheese, grated

2 tablespoons sliced jalapeño peppers from a jar

2 tablespoons coriander leaves

ready-made fresh tomato salsa, to serve

- Heat the oil, paprika and garlic in a frying pan, add the chicken and fry over a medium heat for 5 minutes until the chicken is cooked through. Remove from the pan, then wipe the pan clean with kitchen paper.

- Place the tortillas on a board and cover one half of each tortilla with cheese, cooked chicken, jalapeño peppers and coriander. Fold each tortilla to enclose the filling.

- Heat the frying pan until hot, add the tortilla sandwiches and cook for 2 minutes on each side, until crisp and the cheese starts to melt.

- Serve the quesadillas, cut into wedges, with tomato salsa.

---

1 Chicken Tortilla Toasties

Place 2 soft flour tortillas on a board. Sprinkle over 125 g (4 oz) grated Cheddar cheese, top with 125 g (4 oz) shop-bought ready-cooked chicken, sliced, and a few teaspoons of ready-made spicy tomato salsa. Cover with 2 more tortillas. Cook in a hot frying pan, one tortilla sandwich at a time, for 2 minutes on each side until hot. Cut into wedges and serve with extra salsa and soured cream.

3 Smoky Chicken Quesadillas with Sweetcorn Salsa

 To make the salsa, mix together 125 g (4 oz) canned sweetcorn, 1 chopped spring onion, 1 tablespoon chopped coriander leaves and 1 tablespoon sweet chilli sauce. Set aside. Mix together ½ teaspoon smoked paprika and ½ teaspoon Cajun seasoning in a bowl, add 150 g (5 oz) chicken mini-fillets and toss well to coat. Heat 1 tablespoon olive oil in a frying pan, add the chicken and fry for 5 minutes until cooked through. Remove from the pan, then wipe the pan clean. Sprinkle 125 g (4 oz) grated Cheddar cheese over 2 soft flour tortillas, then top with the cooked chicken, 2 tablespoons sliced jalapeño peppers from a jar and 2 tablespoons coriander leaves. Cover with 2 more tortillas. Cook the tortilla sandwiches in the frying pan, one at a time, for 2–3 minutes on each side. Cut into wedges and serve with the salsa.

30 Sticky Soy Chicken with Fruity Oriental Salad

Serves 4

2 tablespoons clear honey

3 tablespoons tomato ketchup

2 tablespoons vegetable oil

2 tablespoons soy sauce

2 teaspoons sweet chilli sauce

8 chicken thighs, about 75–100 g
(3–3½ oz) each

For the salad

2 Little Gem lettuces, shredded

1 red onion, thinly sliced

8 radishes, sliced

1 orange, peel and pith removed,
halved and sliced

2 tablespoons soy sauce

4 tablespoons orange juice

2 tablespoons olive oil

- Mix together the honey, ketchup, vegetable oil, soy sauce and sweet chilli sauce in a large bowl. Cut a few slashes across each chicken thigh and coat in the honey mixture. Place in a foil-lined roasting tin and cook in a preheated oven, 200°C (400°F), Gas Mark 6, for 25 minutes, or until cooked through.

- Meanwhile, to make the salad, place the lettuce leaves in a salad bowl with the onion, radishes and orange slices. Mix together the soy sauce, orange juice and olive oil in a bowl, then pour over the salad. Serve with the chicken.

---

10 Spicy Chicken with Soy and Pineapple

Noodles Heat 2 x 554 g (1¼ lb) packs ready-cooked hot and spicy chicken wings in a microwave according to the packet instructions. Meanwhile, cook 300 g (10 oz) medium egg noodles in a large saucepan of lightly salted boiling water for 3 minutes, then drain and toss with 4 drained canned pineapple rings, finely chopped, 2 tablespoons soy sauce, 4 teaspoons sesame seeds and 4 thinly sliced spring onions. Serve with the chicken and Chinese plum sauce for dipping.

20 Sticky Soy Chicken and Pineapple

Skewers Mix together 2 tablespoons clear honey, 3 tablespoons tomato ketchup, 2 tablespoons vegetable oil, 4 tablespoons soy sauce and 2 teaspoons sweet chilli sauce in a large bowl. Add 400 g (13 oz) skinless chicken breast fillets, cut into bite-sized chunks, and stir well to coat. Thread the chicken on to 8 metal skewers, alternating with chunks of fresh or canned pineapple. Cook on a foil-lined grill rack under a preheated medium grill for about 10 minutes, turning occasionally, until the chicken is cooked through and lightly charred. Meanwhile, cook 2 x 120 g (4 oz) packets savoury rice according to the packet instructions. Serve with the chicken skewers, sprinkled with strips of spring onion.

MID-CHIC-JEE

30 Caribbean Chicken with Rice and Peas

Serves 2

2 teaspoons jerk seasoning

1 teaspoon peeled and grated
   fresh root ginger

juice of 1 lime

2 boneless, skinless chicken
   breasts, about 150 g (5 oz) each

3 tablespoons vegetable oil

1 small onion, chopped

1 garlic clove, crushed

150 g (5 oz) long grain rice

175 ml (6 fl oz) hot chicken stock

175 ml (6 fl oz) coconut milk

200 g (7 oz) can red kidney
   beans, rinsed and drained

50 g (2 oz) frozen or canned
   sweetcorn

few thyme sprigs, plus extra to
   garnish

lime wedges, to serve

- Mix together the jerk seasoning, ginger and lime juice in a non-metallic bowl. Cut a few slashes across each chicken breast and coat in the mixture. Heat 2 tablespoons of the oil in a frying pan, add the chicken and cook over a medium heat for 15–20 minutes, turning occasionally, until cooked through.

- Meanwhile, heat the remaining oil in a pan, add the onion and garlic and cook for 2 minutes until slightly softened. Add the rice, stock and coconut milk and bring to the boil, then reduce the heat, cover and simmer for 15–20 minutes until the liquid has been absorbed and the rice is tender, adding the kidney beans, sweetcorn and thyme sprigs for the final 5 minutes.

- Slice the chicken and serve with the rice and lime wedges, garnished with a few sprigs of thyme.

---

10 Quick Caribbean Chicken

Heat 1 tablespoon oil in a frying pan, add 200 g (7 oz) chicken mini-fillets and stir-fry over a high heat for 2–3 minutes, or until golden. Reduce the heat and stir in 3 tablespoons jerk barbecue sauce and the juice of 1 lime. Add a 250 g (8 oz) pack ready-cooked rice, a 200 g (7 oz) can kidney beans, rinsed and drained, and 50 g (2 oz) canned or frozen sweetcorn and heat through until piping hot. Serve sprinkled with thyme leaves.

20 Caribbean Chicken, Rice and Pea Pot

Heat 1 tablespoon vegetable oil in a saucepan, add 1 chopped onion, 1 crushed garlic clove and 4 chopped boneless, skinless chicken thighs (about 125 g/4 oz each) and fry for 3–4 minutes. Add 2 teaspoons jerk seasoning, 150 g (5 oz) long-grain rice, a 200 g (7 oz) can chopped tomatoes, 300 ml (½ pint) hot chicken stock and 2 tablespoons jerk barbecue sauce. Bring to the boil, then reduce the heat, cover and simmer for 15 minutes until the rice and chicken are cooked and the liquid has been absorbed, adding a 200 g (7 oz) can kidney beans and 50 g (2 oz) frozen or canned sweetcorn for the final 5 minutes. Serve sprinkled with thyme leaves.

 # Mexican Chicken Burgers with Tomato Salad

Serves 2

2 boneless, skinless chicken
breasts, about 150 g (5 oz)
each, halved horizontally
2 teaspoons fajita seasoning
1 tablespoon olive oil
1 red pepper, cored, quartered
and deseeded
2 soft burger buns, halved
½ avocado, peeled, stoned and
sliced
2 tablespoons soured cream
chopped chives

For the tomato salad

5 cherry tomatoes, halved
½ small red onion, thinly sliced
½ red chilli, deseeded and
chopped
1 tablespoon chopped flat leaf
parsley
squeeze of lime juice
salt and pepper

- Coat the chicken pieces in fajita seasoning, place on a foil-lined grill rack and drizzle with the oil, then add the pepper quarters, skin side up, to the grill rack. Cook under a preheated medium grill for 10–15 minutes, turning occasionally, until the chicken is cooked through and the peppers are soft and lightly charred.

- Meanwhile, make the salad. Mix together all the ingredients in a bowl and season.

- Mix together the soured cream and chives in a small bowl.

- Toast the buns. Then fill with avocado slices, the chicken and the grilled peppers. Top with spoonfuls of tomato salad and soured cream. Serve with the remaining tomato salad.

 Fully Loaded Chicken Nachos

Spread out 200 g (7 oz) tortilla chips in an ovenproof dish. Scatter over 150 g (5 oz) ready-cooked barbecue chicken, chopped. Top with 2 tablespoons tomato salsa. Add 1 tablespoon sliced jalapeño peppers from a jar and sprinkle with 75 g (3 oz) grated Cheddar cheese. Cook under a preheated hot grill for 3–4 minutes until melted and warm. Serve with ready-made guacamole.

Mexican Roasted Chicken Tortillas

Place 2 boneless, skinless chicken breasts, about 150 g (5 oz) each and each cut into 3 pieces, in a roasting tin with 1 red onion, cut into wedges, and 1 red pepper, cored, deseeded and cut into chunks. Drizzle with 2 tablespoons olive oil and season. Roast in a preheated oven, 220°C (425°F), Gas Mark 7, for 20 minutes until cooked through and starting to char.

Meanwhile, peel, stone and mash 1 small ripe avocado. Stir in ½ deseeded and chopped red chilli and season with lime juice and salt. Set aside. Pour 250 g (8 oz) fajita cooking sauce from a jar over the chicken and turn to coat in the sauce. Return to the oven and cook for a further 5 minutes until heated through. Serve with the avocado on warm tortillas with soured cream.

Lemon and Parsley Chicken Skewers

Serves 2

300 g (10 oz) skinless chicken
  breast fillets, cut into chunks
finely grated rind and juice of
  1 lemon
2 tablespoons olive oil
3 tablespoons finely chopped
  parsley
salt and pepper

To serve

rocket and tomato salad
warm pitta breads
211 g (7 oz) tub tzatziki

- Place the chicken in a non-metallic bowl with the lemon rind and juice and the oil and toss well to coat. Stir in the parsley and season well.

- Thread the chicken on to 4 small metal skewers and cook under a preheated hot grill for 6–7 minutes until golden and cooked through, turning once. Serve with a simple rocket and tomato salad, warm pitta breads and spoonfuls of tzatziki.

---

2 Lemon and Parsley-Stuffed Chicken

Make a slit lengthways in the side of 2 boneless chicken breasts, about 150 g (5 oz) each, to form pockets. Thinly slice ½ lemon, then stuff the chicken with the lemon slices. Press a small bunch of parsley into the cavities and season. Tie around each piece once with a piece of kitchen string. Heat 15 g (1 oz) butter and 1 tablespoon olive oil in a frying pan, add the chicken and cook over a medium-high heat for 5–6 minutes on each side until golden and cooked through. Serve with tzatziki and a simple salad.

3 Baked Lemon and Parsley Chicken

Place 4 chicken thighs, about 125 g (4 oz) each, and 1 large roughly chopped courgette in a small roasting tin, scatter with 2 tablespoons chopped parsley and season well. Squeeze over the juice of ½ lemon, then cut the remaining lemon half into wedges and scatter around the chicken. Drizzle with 2 tablespoons olive oil, then bake in a preheated oven, 200°C (400°F), Gas Mark 6, for 20–25 minutes, or until golden and cooked through. Meanwhile, mix together 6 tablespoons double cream and 2 tablespoons natural yogurt, then place in a pan with 2 tablespoons chopped mint leaves. Heat for 2 minutes until warm but not boiling. Serve the chicken and courgettes with the sauce spooned over.

20 Creamy Chicken and Tarragon Pasta

Serves 4

250 g (8 oz) penne
4 tablespoons olive oil
500 g (1 lb) skinless chicken
   breast fillets, cut into thin strips
500 g (1 lb) courgettes, cut into
   thin slices
1 large onion, thinly sliced
2 teaspoons crushed garlic
4 tablespoons pine nuts
finely grated rind and juice of
   2 lemons
8 tablespoons chopped tarragon
200 ml (7 fl oz) crème fraîche
salt

To serve

grated Parmesan cheese
simple salad (optional)

- Cook the penne in a large saucepan of lightly salted boiling water for 8–10 minutes, or until just tender.

- Meanwhile, heat the oil in a large frying pan and cook the chicken for 3–4 minutes until starting to turn golden. Add the courgettes and onion and cook for a further 5 minutes until golden and the chicken is cooked through.

- Add the garlic and pine nuts and cook, stirring, for 2 minutes, then add the lemon rind and juice, tarragon and crème fraîche and stir well until hot but not boiling.

- Drain the pasta well, then add to the sauce and toss well to coat. Serve with grated Parmesan and a simple salad, if liked.

 Creamy Chicken and Tarragon Pan-Fry Heat 2 tablespoons olive oil in a large frying pan, add 2 thinly sliced onions and 500 g (1 lb) thinly sliced skinless chicken breast fillets and cook for 5 minutes until golden and cooked through. Add 4 tablespoons chopped tarragon and 2 tablespoons white wine vinegar and cook for a further 1 minute, then stir in 200 ml (7 fl oz) crème fraîche and 2 teaspoons Dijon mustard. Serve hot.

 Baked Chicken with Creamy Tarragon Sauce Make a slit lengthways in the side of 4 boneless chicken breasts, about 150 g (5 oz) each, with skin on. Open up and season well, then fill each with 2 tarragon sprigs and close up. Place in a large roasting tin with 500 g (1 lb) thickly sliced courgettes and roast in a preheated oven, 220°C (425°F), Gas Mark 7, for 25 minutes, or until cooked through. Meanwhile, heat 2 tablespoons olive oil in a frying pan, add 4 small finely chopped shallots and cook for 3–4 minutes until softened. Add 4 tablespoons chopped tarragon and 2 tablespoons white wine vinegar and cook for a few seconds, then stir in 200 ml (7 fl oz) crème fraîche and 2 teaspoons Dijon mustard and heat through for 1 minute. Serve the chicken with the sauce spooned over.

30 Greek Chicken Stifado

Serves 2

3 tablespoons olive oil

2 chicken quarters

2 shallots, peeled and cut in half

1 fennel bulb, trimmed and cut into slim wedges

400 g (13 oz) can artichokes, drained and halved

50 g (2 oz) kalamata olives, pitted

3 tablespoons sun-dried tomato paste

2 tomatoes, roughly chopped

1 tablespoon rosemary leaves

300 ml (½ pint) hot chicken stock

warm crusty bread, to serve (optional)

- Heat the oil in a large frying pan, add the chicken, skin side down, shallots and fennel wedges and cook over a medium-high heat for 10 minutes until the chicken is golden.

- Turn the chicken over and add the artichokes, olives, tomato paste, tomatoes, rosemary and stock and stir well, then cover tightly and simmer for 15–20 minutes until the chicken is cooked through and the tomatoes have softened, adding a little water if the sauce is too thick. Serve with warm crusty bread, if liked, to mop up the juices.

 Chicken, Artichoke and Olive Pan-Fry

Heat 2 tablespoons olive oil in a large frying pan, add 300 g (10 oz) thinly sliced skinless chicken breast fillets and cook over a high heat until golden, then add 1 teaspoon rosemary leaves, a 400 g (13 oz) can artichokes, drained, 75 g (3 oz) pitted black olives and a 300 g (10 oz) jar tomato pasta sauce with vegetables and cook for 5 minutes until piping hot and the chicken is cooked through. Serve with ready-cooked rice or warm crusty bread to mop up the juices.

 Chicken, Artichoke and Olive Pasta

Heat 2 tablespoons olive oil in a large frying pan, add 1 trimmed and finely sliced fennel bulb and 300 g (10 oz) thinly sliced skinless chicken breast fillets and cook for 5 minutes until the fennel is softened and the chicken is cooked through. Add 6 tablespoons sun-dried tomato paste, a 400 g (13 oz) can artichokes, drained and halved, 75 g (3 oz) pitted black olives and 150 ml (¼ pint) water and bring to the boil, stirring, then reduce the heat, cover and simmer for 5 minutes.

Meanwhile, cook 200 g (7 oz) penne in a saucepan of lightly salted boiling water for 8–10 minutes, or until just tender. Drain the pasta well, then add to the sauce and stir well to coat. Serve with plenty of grated Parmesan cheese.

30 Thyme-Roasted Chicken and Carrots

Serves 4

8 chicken thighs, about 100–125 g
(3½–4 oz) each
2 large red onions, cut into
wedges
2 lemons, cut into wedges
350 g (11½ oz) baby chantenay
carrots
4 tablespoons olive oil
6 tablespoons balsamic vinegar
6 tablespoons thyme leaves
300 ml (½ pint) hot chicken stock
pepper
crusty bread or mashed potatoes,
to serve

- Place the chicken thighs, onions, lemon wedges, carrots, oil, vinegar and thyme in a large bowl and toss together with plenty of pepper. Tip into a large, shallow baking dish and roast in a preheated oven, 220°C (425°F), Gas Mark 7, for 15 minutes.

- Pour in the stock, then return to the oven and cook for a further 10 minutes, or until the chicken is golden and cooked through. Serve with warm crusty bread to mop up the juices, or mashed potatoes, if liked.

 Pan-Fried Chicken, Carrots and Thyme Heat 50 g (2 oz) butter in a large frying pan, add 500 g (1 lb) halved baby chantenay carrots and 500 g (1 lb) thinly sliced skinless chicken breast fillets and cook over a medium heat for 5 minutes until the chicken is cooked through and the carrots are just tender, then add 300 ml (½ pint) hot chicken stock, 4 tablespoons thyme leaves and 2 tablespoons wholegrain mustard and cook for a further 2 minutes. Serve with warm crusty bread.

 Sticky Chicken and Carrots with Thyme Heat 50 g (2 oz) butter and 2 tablespoons olive oil in a large frying pan, add 2 large thinly sliced red onions and 500 g (1 lb) thinly sliced skinless chicken breast fillets and cook for 8–10 minutes until golden and softened. Meanwhile, cook 500 g (1 lb) chantenay carrots, halved lengthways, in a large saucepan of boiling water for 5 minutes until just tender. Drain well and add to the chicken with 4 tablespoons balsamic vinegar, then stir and cook gently for a further 5 minutes until the chicken and carrots are cooked through, adding 4 tablespoons chopped thyme leaves for the final 1 minute. Serve hot.

Chicken and Chorizo with Green Lentils

Serves 2

1 tablespoon olive oil
1 small onion, thinly sliced
125 g (4 oz) chorizo sausage, thinly sliced
300 g (10 oz) skinless chicken breast fillets, cubed
250 g (8 oz) pack ready-cooked green lentils
2 tablespoons thyme leaves
150 ml (¼ pint) hot chicken stock
1 tablespoon Dijon mustard
salt and pepper
crusty bread, to serve (optional)

- Heat the oil in a large frying pan, add the onion, chorizo and chicken and cook over a medium-high heat for 5–7 minutes, stirring occasionally, until golden and the chicken is cooked through.

- Add the lentils, thyme, stock and mustard and stir well to combine, then cook for a further 2 minutes until boiling. Season well with pepper and a little salt to taste. Serve with crusty bread, if liked.

 Chicken and Chorizo Kebabs with Lentil Purée Thread 125 g (4 oz) thickly sliced chorizo sausage, 250 g (8 oz) cubed skinless chicken breast fillets and 1 onion, cut into wedges, on to 4 metal skewers. Brush with 1 tablespoon olive oil and season. Cook under a preheated medium grill for 8–10 minutes, turning frequently, until cooked through. Meanwhile, place a 250 g (8 oz) pack ready-cooked green lentils and 6 tablespoons hot chicken stock in a saucepan and bring to the boil. Add 1 tablespoon thyme leaves and season, then transfer to a food processor and whizz until smooth. Serve with the kebabs.

 Chicken, Chorizo and Lentil Soup Heat 1 tablespoon olive oil in a large saucepan, add 1 roughly chopped onion, 125 g (4 oz) diced chorizo sausage and 150 g (5 oz) roughly diced skinless chicken breast fillets and cook for 4–5 minutes until golden and the chicken is cooked through. Add 175 g (6 oz) green lentils and 500 ml (17 fl oz) hot chicken stock and bring to the boil. Reduce the heat, cover and simmer for 20 minutes until the lentils are tender. Stir in 1 tablespoon Dijon mustard and season well. Transfer the mixture to a food processor and whizz until almost smooth. Serve with crusty bread.

MID-CHIC-QYG

Chicken, Pancetta and Mushroom Carbonara

Serves 2

250 g (8 oz) linguine
2 tablespoons olive oil
300 g (10 oz) skinless chicken
  breast fillets, cut into chunks
125 g (4 oz) chestnut mushrooms,
  quartered
125 g (4 oz) pancetta, cut into
  small pieces
2 egg yolks
300 ml (½ pint) double cream
50 g (2 oz) grated Parmesan
  cheese
salt and pepper

- Cook the linguine in a large saucepan of lightly salted boiling water for 8–10 minutes, or until just tender. Drain well, then return to the pan.

- Meanwhile, heat the oil in a frying pan, add the chicken, mushrooms and pancetta and cook over a high heat for 5–7 minutes until golden and cooked through.

- Mix together the egg yolks, cream and Parmesan in a bowl until smooth and season well.

- Add the cooked chicken mixture to the drained linguine, then gently pour the cream mixture over the pasta and, using 2 wooden spoons, toss over a very low heat until hot and thickened, taking care not to overcook.

 Creamy Chicken, Pancetta and Mushroom Pasta Cook 300 g (10 oz) fresh linguine in a saucepan of lightly salted boiling water for 3 minutes, or until just tender, then drain. Meanwhile, heat 3 tablespoons olive oil in a frying pan, add 125 g (4 oz) finely chopped pancetta, 175 g (6 oz) sliced mushrooms and 150 g (5 oz) shop-bought ready-cooked chicken breast, thinly sliced, and cook over a high heat for 3–4 minutes. Add the drained pasta with 150 ml (¼ pint) double cream and 4 tablespoons grated Parmesan cheese and toss for 1 minute to coat, then serve.

 Chicken, Pancetta and Mushroom Pasta Bake Cook 250 g (8 oz) penne in a large saucepan of lightly salted boiling water for 8–10 minutes, or until just tender, then drain and return to the pan. Meanwhile, heat 4 tablespoons olive oil in a frying pan, add 300 g (10 oz) cubed skinless chicken breast fillets, 125 g (4 oz) thinly sliced chestnut mushrooms and 125 g (4 oz) roughly chopped pancetta and cook over a high heat for 5–7 minutes until golden and cooked through. Add to the drained pasta and toss well. Add 300 ml (½ pint) double cream and 50 g (2 oz) grated Parmesan cheese and toss well to coat. Season well, then transfer to a medium gratin dish. Slice a small garlic baguette, then place the slices over the pasta. Scatter with 125 g (4 oz) grated Cheddar cheese. Bake in a preheated oven, 200°C (400°F), Gas Mark 6, for 10 minutes, then transfer to a preheated hot grill and cook for 2–3 minutes until piping hot and golden. Serve with a simple salad.

MID-CHIC-BAX

Warm Chicken, Med Veg and Bulgar Wheat Salad

Serves 4

6 tablespoons olive oil

1 large courgette, cut into thick slices

1 large red onion, cut into slim wedges

1 red pepper, cored, deseeded and cut into chunks

½ small aubergine, cut into small chunks

1 garlic clove, thinly sliced

150 g (5 oz) bulgar wheat

4 boneless, skinless chicken breasts, about 200 g (7 oz) each

4 tablespoons chopped parsley

salt and pepper

- Heat 5 tablespoons of the oil in a large frying pan, add the courgette, onion, red pepper, aubergine and garlic and cook over a high heat for 15–20 minutes, stirring almost continuously, until golden and softened.

- Meanwhile, cook the bulgar wheat in a saucepan of lightly salted boiling water for 15 minutes until tender.

- While the bulgar wheat is cooking, brush the remaining oil over the chicken breasts and season well. Heat a large griddle pan until smoking, add the chicken and cook over a high heat for 4–5 minutes on each side, or until golden and cooked through. Remove from the heat and thinly slice diagonally.

- Drain the bulgar wheat. Place in a large bowl, toss with the parsley and season. Add the hot vegetables and chicken, toss together and serve.

Warm Chicken and Med Veg Pittas

Mix together 600 g (1 lb 5 oz) thinly sliced skinless chicken breast fillets and 2 tablespoons olive oil in a large bowl and season well. Heat a large griddle pan until hot, add the chicken and 2 thinly sliced courgettes and cook over a high heat for 5 minutes, or until cooked through. Add 2 chopped tomatoes and cook for a further 2 minutes. Serve in 4 warm pitta breads with a handful of rocket leaves in each and spoonfuls of natural yogurt, if liked.

Chicken and Med Veg Kebabs with Herby Bulgar Wheat

Cook 200 g (7oz) bulgar wheat in a large saucepan of lightly salted boiling water for 15 minutes. Meanwhile, thread 300 g (10 oz) cubed skinless chicken breast fillets, 1 cored, deseeded and cubed red pepper, 2 small thickly sliced courgettes and 2 red onions, cut into wedges, on to 8 metal skewers. Lightly brush with olive oil and season well. Cook under a preheated medium grill for 8–10 minutes until golden and cooked through. Drain the bulgar wheat and place in a large bowl with 8 tablespoons chopped parsley or chives, or both, and toss to mix. Season well, then serve topped with the kebabs.

2 Chicken, Potato and Spinach Pan-Fry

Serves 2

6 tablespoons olive oil

425 g (14 oz) potatoes, peeled and cubed

250 g (8 oz) boneless, skinless chicken thighs, cut into thin strips

1 garlic clove, thinly sliced

75 g (3 oz) prosciutto, torn into pieces

2 tablespoons chopped sage leaves, plus extra leaves to garnish (optional)

150 g (5 oz) baby spinach leaves

200 ml (7 fl oz) crème fraîche

1 tablespoon wholegrain mustard

- Heat the oil in a large frying pan, add the potatoes and cook over a high heat for 5 minutes until starting to turn golden in places.

- Add the chicken and garlic and cook for 5 minutes until cooked through, then add the prosciutto and sage and cook for a further 2 minutes until the prosciutto is golden and the potatoes are tender. Add the spinach and fry, stirring, for 1 minute until wilted.

- Mix together the crème fraîche and mustard in a bowl, then spoon into the pan and cook for 2 minutes until piping hot. Serve scattered with extra sage leaves, if liked.

 Simple Chicken and Spinach with Mash

Heat 2 tablespoons olive oil in a frying pan, add 250 g (8 oz) diced boneless, skinless chicken thighs and 1 sliced garlic clove and cook for 4–5 minutes until cooked through. Add 75 g (3 oz) torn prosciutto and cook for a further 2 minutes, then add 1 tablespoon chopped sage leaves and 150 g (5 oz) baby spinach leaves and cook for 2 minutes. Add 200 ml (7 fl oz) crème fraîche and stir for 1 minute until hot. Serve with ready-cooked mashed potatoes.

 Chicken, Spinach and Potato Gratin

Cook 425 g (14 oz) peeled and cubed potatoes in a saucepan of lightly salted boiling water for 8 minutes until tender. Meanwhile, heat 3 tablespoons olive oil in a large frying pan, add 250 g (8 oz) boneless, skinless chicken thighs, cut into thin strips, and 1 thinly sliced garlic clove and cook for 5 minutes until golden. Add 75 g (3 oz) prosciutto, torn into pieces, and 2 tablespoons chopped sage leaves and cook for a further 3 minutes until golden and the chicken is cooked through. Drain the potatoes and add to the chicken with 150 g (5 oz) baby spinach leaves, and cook for 2 minutes until wilted. Stir in 200 ml (7 fl oz) crème fraîche and 1 tablespoon wholegrain mustard and toss well. Transfer to a shallow gratin dish and scatter with 125 g (4 oz) grated Cheddar cheese. Cook under a preheated hot grill for 5 minutes until golden and bubbling. Serve with salad, if liked.

3 Roasted Chicken and Spiced Butternut Squash

Serves 2

4 chicken quarters

350 g (11½ oz) pack ready-prepared butternut squash pieces

2 tablespoons olive oil

½ red chilli, deseeded and roughly chopped

1 teaspoon cumin seeds

1 teaspoon ground coriander

½ teaspoon ground paprika

2 tablespoons chopped sage leaves

salt and pepper

sugar snap peas, to serve (optional)

- Place the chicken in a roasting tin and season well. Mix together the remaining ingredients in a bowl, ensuring the oil and spices thoroughly coat the squash pieces, then arrange around the chicken.

- Place in a preheated oven, 220°C (425°F), Gas Mark 7, for 25 minutes, or until the chicken is cooked through and the squash is soft and lightly charred in places. Serve with blanched sugar snap peas, if liked.

 Spicy Chicken Strips with Sweet Potatoes Pierce 125 g (4 oz) sweet potatoes several times with a knife. Cook in a microwave on High for 8 minutes, or until cooked through. Meanwhile, heat 2 tablespoons olive oil in a frying pan, add 300 g (10 oz) thinly sliced skinless chicken breast fillets and cook over a high heat for 7–8 minutes until golden and cooked through. Add ½ teaspoon chilli powder, ½ teaspoon ground coriander and ½ teaspoon cumin seeds and toss again for 1 minute. Cut open each sweet potato and add a knob of butter to each. Serve with the chicken and a handful of rocket leaves.

 Spiced Chicken and Butternut Soup Heat 1 tablespoon olive oil in a large saucepan, add a 350 g (11½ oz) pack ready-prepared butternut squash pieces, chopped into smaller pieces, ½ red chilli, deseeded and roughly chopped, and 150 g (5 oz) roughly chopped skinless chicken breast fillets and cook for 5 minutes, stirring occasionally. Add 1 teaspoon cumin seeds, 1 teaspoon ground coriander and 600 ml (1 pint) hot chicken stock and bring to the boil. Reduce the heat, cover and simmer for 12 minutes until the squash is tender and the chicken cooked through. Transfer the mixture to a food processor and whizz until smooth. Scatter with chopped sage leaves, if liked, and serve with warm crusty wholemeal bread.

20 Oriental Chicken Satay Stir-Fry

Serves 2

2 tablespoons sesame oil

300 g (10 oz) skinless chicken breast fillets, cut into long, thick strips

1 bunch of large spring onions, cut in half lengthways

1 orange pepper, cored, deseeded and cut into thick strips

1 head of pak choi, about 175 g (6 oz), leaves separated

boiled rice, to serve (optional)

For the satay sauce

150 ml (¼ pint) boiling water

4 tablespoons smooth peanut butter

2 tablespoons soy sauce

1 tablespoon sweet chilli sauce

- Heat the oil in a large wok or frying pan, add the chicken strips and stir-fry over a high heat for 5 minutes until golden in places. Add the spring onions and stir-fry for a further 3 minutes.

- Add the orange pepper and continue to stir-fry for 3 minutes until the chicken and vegetables are cooked through. Add the pak choi and cook for 1 minute. Remove from the heat.

- To make the sauce, place the measurement water in a small saucepan with the remaining ingredients and bring to the boil, stirring with a balloon whisk until smooth. Pour into the wok with the chicken and vegetables and toss to coat. Serve immediately with rice, if liked.

---

10 Quick Chicken Satay Stir-Fry

Heat 1 tablespoon sesame oil in a wok, add 250 g (8 oz) chicken mini-fillets and stir-fry over a high heat for 5 minutes until golden. Add a 300 g (10 oz) pack ready-prepared stir-fry vegetables and 4 spring onions, roughly chopped, and stir-fry for a further 2–3 minutes until tender. In a jug, mix together 1 tablespoon soy sauce, 2 tablespoons smooth peanut butter and 4 tablespoons boiling water. Pour into the wok and toss and cook for a further 1 minute. Serve hot.

30 Satay Chicken Skewers with Oriental Veg Stir-Fry

Place 2 heaped tablespoons smooth peanut butter, 1 tablespoon soy sauce, 1 tablespoon sweet chilli sauce and 6 tablespoons water in a small saucepan and heat gently for about 2 minutes, stirring continuously until smooth, thick and warm. Place 300 g (10 oz) skinless chicken breast fillets, cut into strips, 1 tablespoon sesame oil, 2 tablespoons soy sauce and 1 cm (½ inch) piece of fresh root ginger, peeled and grated, in a bowl and mix well. Leave to marinate for 5 minutes. Thread the chicken on to 4 pre-soaked wooden skewers and place on a foil-lined grill rack. Cook under a preheated hot grill for 7–8 minutes until cooked through, turning halfway through cooking. Meanwhile, heat 1 tablespoon sesame oil in a wok or frying pan, add 1 shredded head of pak choi, 1 cored, deseeded and thinly sliced orange pepper and 6 roughly chopped spring onions and stir-fry for 3–4 minutes until softened but still retaining their shape. Serve with the skewers and satay sauce.

MID-CHIC-KUA

Spicy Chicken and Plantain with Caribbean Sauce

Serves 2

1 tablespoon sunflower oil

1 small plantain, about 375 g (12 oz), peeled and thinly sliced

250 g (8 oz) skinless chicken breast fillets, thinly sliced

2 tomatoes, roughly chopped

150 ml (¼ pint) coconut milk

150 ml (¼ pint) passata

2 tablespoons Jamaican jerk seasoning

1 tablespoon thyme leaves, to garnish (optional)

ready-cooked rice, to serve

- Heat the oil in a frying pan, add the plantain and cook over a high heat for 2 minutes, stirring occasionally, then remove from the pan with a slotted spoon and set aside. Add the chicken to the pan and cook for a further 5 minutes, stirring occasionally, until the chicken is golden and cooked through. Return the plantain to the pan.

- Add the tomatoes, coconut milk, passata and jerk seasoning and bring to the boil, then cook for 2 minutes until piping hot. Spoon into 2 warm serving bowls and scatter with the thyme leaves, if using. Serve with rice.

Spicy Chicken with Plantain Chips

Heat 2 tablespoons oil in a frying pan, add 300 g (10 oz) sliced skinless chicken breast fillets and 1 chopped onion and cook over a high heat for 5 minutes. Add 1 teaspoon each of ground cumin, ground ginger, ground paprika and ready-minced garlic and a 400 g (13 oz) can chopped tomatoes and bring to the boil. Reduce the heat, cover and simmer for 10 minutes. Meanwhile, heat 150 ml (¼ pint) sunflower oil in a deep saucepan until a cube of bread browns in 30 seconds. Cut ½ peeled plantain into slices and deep-fry for about 1 minute until crisp and golden. Remove with a slotted spoon and drain on kitchen paper. Season and serve with the chicken.

Spiced Chicken and Plantain Stew

Heat 2 tablespoons olive oil in a large frying pan, add 4 small chicken thighs and cook over a medium heat for 5 minutes, turning once. Add 1 roughly chopped onion and cook for a further 3 minutes, then add 1 crushed garlic clove, 1 cored, deseeded and roughly chopped red pepper, 250 g (8 oz) peeled and sliced plantain and 125 g (4 oz) okra, trimmed and cut in half, and cook for a further 3–4 minutes until the vegetables are starting to soften and the chicken turns golden. Add ½ teaspoon each of ground cloves, ground cinnamon and ground nutmeg and 1 teaspoon dried thyme and stir to coat.

Pour in a 400 g (13 oz) can chopped tomatoes and 150 ml (¼ pint) hot chicken stock and bring to the boil, then reduce the heat, cover and simmer for 15–18 minutes, turning the chicken once, until it is cooked through and the sauce slightly reduced. Serve with rice mixed with kidney beans.

3⟨ Chicken Jalfrezi

Serves 2

2 tablespoons sunflower oil

300 g (10 oz) skinless chicken breast fillets, cut into pieces

1 onion, cut into slim wedges

1 small green pepper, cored, deseeded and cut into chunks

1 green chilli, deseeded and finely chopped

1 teaspoon ground cumin

1 teaspoon garam masala

½ teaspoon turmeric

2 tomatoes, cut into wedges

2 tablespoons natural yogurt

200 ml (7 fl oz) water

warm naan breads, to serve

- Heat the oil in a large frying pan, add the chicken, onion and green pepper and cook over a medium heat for 10 minutes until starting to turn golden. Add the chilli and spices and cook for 2–3 minutes, then add the tomatoes and cook for a further 3 minutes.

- Stir in the yogurt, then pour in the measurement water, cover and simmer very gently for 10 minutes until the chicken is cooked through and the flavours have infused, stirring occasionally and adding a little more water if necessary. Serve with warm naan breads to mop up the juices.

1⟨ Speedy Chicken Curry

Heat 2 tablespoons sunflower oil in a frying pan over a high heat, add 300 g (10 oz) very thinly sliced skinless chicken breast fillets and cook for 5 minutes until golden and cooked through. Add ½ deseeded and roughly chopped red chilli and cook for a further 1 minute, then add a 300 g (10 oz) jar jalfrezi sauce and heat through for 2–3 minutes. Stir in 4 tablespoons natural yogurt and serve with ready-cooked pilau rice, if liked.

2⟨ Spicy Chicken Stir-Fry

Heat 1 tablespoon sunflower oil in a wok, add 300 g (10 oz) roughly chopped skinless chicken breast fillets and 1 large onion, cut into slim wedges, and stir-fry over a medium-high heat for 5–6 minutes until the chicken is golden and cooked through and the onions are softened. Add ½ deseeded and roughly chopped green chilli and cook for a further 1 minute, then add a 300 g (10 oz) pack ready-prepared stir-fry vegetables and 2 teaspoons garam masala and stir-fry for 3–4 minutes until the vegetables are softened. Spoon into chapattis, roll up and serve.

30 Honeyed Chicken and Roasted Rosemary Roots

Serves 4

8 chicken thighs, about 100–125 g
(3½–4 oz) each

600 g (1 lb 5 oz) small parsnips,
peeled and halved lengthways

500 g (1 lb) small carrots,
trimmed and halved lengthways

2 small turnips, about 200 g
(7 oz) each, peeled and cut into
slim wedges

6 tablespoons olive oil

2 tablespoons rosemary leaves

4 tablespoons clear honey

salt and pepper

2 small handfuls of thyme,
to garnish

- Place the chicken in a large roasting tin and season well. Place the vegetables around the chicken, drizzle with the oil and toss. Scatter over the rosemary and season.

- Roast in a preheated oven, 220°C (425°F), Gas Mark 7, for 25 minutes, or until golden and cooked through. Drizzle over the honey and, using 2 spoons, toss well. Return to the oven and cook for a further 2 minutes. Serve scattered with the thyme.

 Simple Honeyed Rosemary Chicken and Roots Heat 4 tablespoons olive oil in a large frying pan, add 500 g (1 lb) thinly sliced skinless chicken breast fillets and 400 g (13 oz) peeled and thinly sliced carrots and cook over a medium heat for 5–7 minutes until golden and cooked through. Add 2 tablespoons roughly chopped rosemary leaves and 150 ml (¼ pint) white wine, stir and leave to boil until almost all the wine evaporates, then add 4 tablespoons clear honey and toss well for 1 minute. Season well, then serve with ready-cooked rice, if liked.

 Rosemary and Honey-Glazed Chicken and Roots Heat 4 tablespoons olive oil in a large frying pan, add 500 g (1 lb) parsnips, peeled and roughly chopped, 2 onions, cut into slim wedges, and 500 g (1 lb) carrots, peeled and roughly chopped, and cook for 5 minutes over a medium heat until just tender. Add 500 g (1 lb) skinless chicken breast fillets, cut into chunks, and cook, turning and stirring, for a further 8–10 minutes until cooked through, reducing the heat if the vegetables become too golden. Add 2 tablespoons chopped rosemary leaves and 4 tablespoons clear honey and toss and stir for 1 minute. Serve hot.

10 Creamy Chicken, Gammon and Leek Pan-Fry

Serves 2

1 tablespoon olive oil
15 g (½ oz) butter
250 g (8 oz) skinless chicken
   breast fillets, cut into chunks
125 g (4 oz) gammon steak,
   cubed
1 leek, trimmed, cleaned and
   thinly sliced
200 ml (7 fl oz) crème fraîche
1 tablespoon wholegrain mustard
1 teaspoon Dijon mustard
ready-cooked rice, mashed
   potatoes or warm crusty bread,
   to serve

- Heat the oil and butter in a frying pan, add the chicken and gammon and cook over a high heat for 5 minutes. Add the leek and cook for a further 3 minutes, stirring almost continuously, until the leek is slightly golden and softened and the chicken is cooked through.

- Mix together the crème fraîche and mustards in a bowl, then stir into the chicken and gammon and heat through for 1 minute until piping hot. Serve with rice, mashed potatoes or warm crusty bread.

 Leek-Stuffed Chicken in Prosciutto Heat 1 tablespoon olive oil in a frying pan, add 1 small trimmed, cleaned and very thinly sliced leek and cook for 3–4 minutes until softened. Make a slit lengthways in 2 boneless, skinless chicken breasts, about 150 g (5 oz) each, to form pockets. Place 1 slice of Gruyère, about 25 g (1 oz), into each pocket, then fill with the leek mixture. Tightly wrap each with 1 slice of prosciutto to secure the filling. Heat 1 tablespoon olive oil in the pan and cook the chicken over a medium heat for 10–12 minutes, turning frequently, until golden and cooked through.

 Creamy Chicken, Gammon and Leek Gratin Heat 2 tablespoons olive oil in a frying pan, add 300 g (10 oz) skinless chicken breast fillets, cut into chunks, and 125 g (4 oz) cubed gammon steak and cook for 5 minutes until starting to turn golden. Add 1 large trimmed, cleaned and sliced leek, and cook for a further 3 minutes until the chicken is cooked through, then set aside. In a separate saucepan, melt 25 g (1 oz) butter, add 25 g (1 oz) plain flour and cook for a few seconds, stirring. Remove from the heat and gradually add 300 ml (½ pint) milk. Return to the heat and bring to the boil, stirring continuously until boiled and thickened. Stir in 1 tablespoon Dijon mustard and 1 tablespoon wholegrain mustard. Stir the chicken and leek mixture into the sauce, then transfer to a shallow ovenproof dish and scatter with 4 tablespoons fresh wholemeal breadcrumbs and 2 tablespoons grated Parmesan cheese. Cook under a preheated hot grill for 2–3 minutes until golden and bubbling.

MID-CHIC-VUO

QuickCook

Fish and Seafood

Recipes listed by cooking time

30

Garlicky Cider Mussels with Chips 128

Pesto Fish Pie 130

Niçoise Pasta Salad 132

Salt, Pepper and Chilli Squid with Chips and Garlic Mayo 134

Ginger and Lime Mackerel with Roasted Veg 136

Baked Anchovy Tomatoes with Spaghetti 138

Smoked Haddock Rarebit Tart 140

Teriyaki Salmon with Sesame Broccoli 142

Thai Crab Cakes with Carrot Noodle Salad 144

Seafood Tagliatelle 146

Asparagus, Lemon and Herb-Stuffed Salmon 148

Prawn Jambalaya 150

Smoked Fish and Fennel Pie 152

Prawn and Coconut Curry 154

Creamy Salmon Pie with Herby Mash 156

Baked Herby Cod with Gruyère and Spinach Mash 158

Thai-Style Fishcakes 160

Chilli Seafood Stew 162

Chilli and Lemon Fishcakes 164

Roasted Garlicky Herb Sea Bass, Fennel and Potatoes 166

Creamy Baked Scallops and Bacon 168

Juicy Cod Burgers with Tartare Sauce 170

Prawn and Crab Spring Rolls 172

Roasted Prosciutto-Wrapped Salmon and Potatoes 174

20

Mussels with Cider and Garlic Sauce 128

Crispy Pesto Baked Cod 130

Tuna and Bean Pasta Salad 132

Polenta Chilli Squid with Lime Mayo 134

Ginger and Lime Mackerel with Fennel Salad and New Potatoes 136

Spaghetti Puttanesca 138

Smoked Haddock Rarebit 140

Teriyaki Salmon with Egg Noodles 142

Quick Thai Crab Cakes with Carrot Salad 144

Simple Seafood Risotto 146

Lemony Salmon and Asparagus 148

Cajun Prawn Rice and Peas 150

Smoked Fish and Fennel Crêpes 152

Prawn and Coconut Pan-Fry 154

10

Pan-Fried Herby
Salmon with Creamy
Mascarpone Sauce   156

Herby Cod with Cheesy
Spinach and Mash Pots   158

Thai Green Fish Curry
with Lime Leaves   160

Spicy Seafood Soup   162

Deep-Fried Chilli Cod
Balls   164

Pan-Fried Herb and Garlic
Sea Bass and Fennel   166

Griddled Scallops in
Bacon   168

Fish Finger Rolls with
Tartare Sauce   170

Gingered Prawn and
Crab Rice   172

Grilled Salmon with Creamy
Prosciutto Sauce   174

Mussel, Garlic and
Cider Tagliatelle   128

Fish Finger Baguettes
with Pesto Mayo   130

Tuna and Bean
Pitta Pockets   132

Crispy Squid with
Chilli Dipping Sauce   134

Pan-Fried Ginger and
Lime Mackerel with
Roasted Veg Couscous   136

Anchovy Tomato Toasts 138

Quick Hot-Smoked
Haddock Rarebits   140

Teriyaki Salmon Stir-Fry 142

Thai Crab and Carrot
Salad   144

Creamy Seafood Pasta   146

Grilled Lemon Salmon
with Asparagus   148

Cajun-Spiced Prawns   150

Smoked Fish and
Fennel Pan-Fry   152

Chilled Coconut Soup
with Sizzling Prawns   154

Creamy Salmon with
Herbs   156

Pan-Fried Cod with
Herby Cheese Mash   158

Thai Prawn Stir-Fry   160

Seafood, Chilli and
Tomato Pan-Fry   162

Chilli and Lemon
Tuna Balls   164

Sea Bass Fillets with
Garlic and Herb Butter 166

Scallop, Bacon and
Pine Nut Pan-Fry   168

Cod Rolls with
Tartare Sauce   170

Oriental Prawn and
Crab Stir-Fry   172

Pan-Fried Prosciutto-
Wrapped Salmon   174

Mussels with Cider and Garlic Sauce

Serves 2

1 kg (2 lb) live mussels
15 g (½ oz) butter
1 garlic clove, chopped
100 ml (3½ fl oz) dry cider
2 tablespoons double cream
1 tablespoon chopped thyme
leaves
salt and pepper
crusty bread, to serve

- Wash the mussels under cold running water and discard any that are open or don't shut when tapped. Pull off any fibrous 'beards' and remove any barnacles, then rinse again.

- Heat the butter in a large saucepan, add the garlic and cook gently for 1 minute. Tip in the mussels and add the cider. Bring to the boil, then cover and cook for 3–4 minutes, shaking the pan occasionally until the mussels have opened.

- Using a slotted spoon, transfer the mussels to 2 warm serving bowls, discarding any that remain closed. Reheat the pan juices, add the cream and thyme and season. Pour over the mussels and serve with plenty of crusty bread.

 ### Mussel, Garlic and Cider Tagliatelle

Place a 560 g (1¼ lb) pack ready-cooked mussels in garlic butter in a large saucepan, add 100 ml (3½ fl oz) dry cider and 2 tablespoons crème fraîche and heat through for 5 minutes until piping hot. Meanwhile, cook 300 g (10 oz) fresh egg tagliatelle in a saucepan of lightly salted boiling water for 3 minutes, or until just tender. Drain, then add to the mussel pan and stir to coat in the sauce. Serve sprinkled with chopped parsley.

 ### Garlicky Cider Mussels with Chips

Cut 2 scrubbed baking potatoes into chips, place on a baking sheet and drizzle over 1 tablespoon olive oil. Season and bake in a preheated oven, 200°C (400°F), Gas Mark 6, for 25 minutes, turning occasionally, until golden and cooked. Meanwhile, wash 1 kg (2 lb) live mussels under cold running water and discard any that don't shut when tapped. Pull off any fibrous 'beards' and remove any barnacles, then rinse again. Heat 15 g (½ oz) butter in a large saucepan, add 2 chopped garlic cloves and 2 chopped shallots and cook for 1 minute, then tip in the mussels and add 100 ml (3½ fl oz) dry cider. Bring to the boil, cover and cook for 3–4 minutes, shaking the pan occasionally until the mussels have opened. Using a slotted spoon, transfer the mussels to 2 warm serving bowls, discarding any that remain closed. Reheat the pan juices and stir in 2 tablespoons crème fraîche and 1 tablespoon chopped parsley. Season and pour over the mussels. Serve with the chips.

MID-FISH-DIL

Crispy Pesto Baked Cod

Serves 2

2 pieces of skinless cod fillet, about 175 g (6 oz) each

4 teaspoons pesto

25 g (1 oz) fresh white breadcrumbs

25 g (1 oz) grated Parmesan cheese

8 cherry tomatoes, halved

8 black olives, pitted

2 tablespoons olive oil

salt and pepper

To serve

new potatoes

peas

- Place the fish on a baking tray and spread the pesto over the top. Mix together the breadcrumbs and Parmesan in a bowl, then season. Spoon the breadcrumb mixture over the pesto.

- Add the tomatoes and olives to the baking tray and drizzle over the oil. Bake in a preheated oven, 220°C (425°F), Gas Mark 7, for 15 minutes, or until the fish is cooked through. Serve with new potatoes and peas.

Fish Finger Baguettes with Pesto Mayo Cook 6 fish fingers under a preheated medium grill for 8 minutes, turning once, until golden and cooked through. Meanwhile, cut 2 x 15 cm (6 inch) pieces of French bread in half and toast the cut sides. Mix 2 teaspoons pesto with 2 tablespoons mayonnaise in a small bowl, then spread over the toasted bread. Top with salad leaves and the fish fingers.

Pesto Fish Pie Heat 1 tablespoon olive oil in a frying pan, add 300 g (10 oz) skinless cod fillet and fry for 8–10 minutes, turning occasionally, until cooked through. Remove from the pan. Add 1 tablespoon pesto and 4 tablespoons crème fraîche to the pan and heat through, stirring, then break the fish into chunks, add to the sauce and simmer for a few minutes. Meanwhile, heat a 425 g (14 oz) pack fresh ready-cooked mashed potatoes in a microwave according to the packet instructions. Spoon the fish and sauce into a flameproof dish and spoon the mashed potatoes over the top. Sprinkle over 25 g (1 oz) grated Cheddar cheese, then cook under a preheated medium grill for 5 minutes until crisp and golden. Serve with peas.

Tuna and Bean Pasta Salad

Serves 2

150 g (5 oz) penne

75 g (3 oz) green beans, trimmed and halved

200 g (7 oz) can tuna steak in sunflower oil, drained and broken into chunks

200 g (7 oz) canned kidney beans, rinsed and drained

50 g (2 oz) antipasti roasted peppers from a jar, drained and chopped

2 spring onions, chopped

1 tablespoon balsamic vinegar

½ teaspoon Dijon mustard

3 tablespoons olive oil

salt and pepper

- Cook the penne in a saucepan of lightly salted boiling water for 10 minutes, or until just tender, adding the green beans for the final 5 minutes. Drain and rinse under cold running water, then drain again.

- Place the pasta and green beans in a bowl with the tuna, kidney beans, peppers and spring onions.

- In a small bowl, whisk together the vinegar, mustard and oil. Season, then pour the dressing over the salad and toss lightly to mix.

 Tuna and Bean Pitta Pockets

Drain a 200 g (7 oz) can tuna steak in sunflower oil and break into chunks. Place in a bowl and add 200 g (7 oz) canned five bean salad, rinsed and drained, 2 chopped spring onions and 8 pitted and chopped black olives. Spoon over 3 tablespoons ready-made French dressing and mix well. Warm 2 pitta breads, cut in half and open out into pockets. Fill with the tuna and bean mixture and some Little Gem lettuce leaves.

 Niçoise Pasta Salad

Cook 150 g (5 oz) penne or other pasta in a saucepan of lightly salted boiling water for 10 minutes, or until just tender, adding 75 g (3 oz) trimmed green beans for the final 5 minutes. Drain and rinse under cold running water, then drain again. In a separate small saucepan, boil 2 eggs for 8 minutes, then drain and leave to cool in cold water. Arrange the pasta and beans on a serving plate. Add a 200 g (7 oz) can tuna steak, drained and broken into chunks, 2 tomatoes, cut into wedges, and 8 black olives. Shell the eggs, cut in half and place on the salad. Mix together 1 tablespoon balsamic vinegar, ½ teaspoon Dijon mustard and 3 tablespoons olive oil in a bowl. Season and drizzle over the salad.

MID-FISH-LUT

30 Salt, Pepper and Chilli Squid with Chips and Garlic Mayo

Serves 4

4 baking potatoes, about 175 g
(6 oz) each, scrubbed

4 tablespoons olive oil

2 garlic cloves, crushed

8 tablespoons mayonnaise

vegetable or groundnut oil,
for deep-frying

625 g (1 lb 6 oz) ready-prepared
squid, sliced

salt and pepper

lemon wedges, to serve

For the batter

150 g (5 oz) plain flour

2 tablespoons cornflour

2 teaspoons coarsely ground
black pepper

1 teaspoon dried chilli flakes

1 teaspoon sea salt flakes

400 ml (14 fl oz) chilled sparkling
water

· Cut the potatoes into chips, toss with the olive oil and season. Spread out over a large baking tray and bake in a preheated oven, 200°C (400°F), Gas Mark 6, for 25 minutes, turning occasionally, until golden and tender.

· Meanwhile, mix together the garlic and mayonnaise in a serving bowl and set aside. Half fill a deep saucepan with vegetable or groundnut oil and heat to 190°C (375°F), or until a cube of bread browns in 30 seconds.

· Make the batter. Place the flour and cornflour in a bowl, add the pepper, chilli flakes and salt flakes and quickly stir in the sparkling water to make a light batter. Do not over-mix – it doesn't matter if it's still a bit lumpy.

· Quickly dip the squid pieces in the batter and drain off the excess. Deep-fry in batches in the hot oil for 2–3 minutes until crisp and golden. Remove with a slotted spoon and drain on kitchen paper. Serve with the chips, garlic mayonnaise and lemon wedges.

 Crispy Squid with Chilli Dipping Sauce

Dust 375 g (12 oz) ready-prepared squid rings in seasoned flour, then shallow-fry, in batches if necessary, in hot vegetable or groundnut oil for 2–3 minutes until crisp and golden. Remove with a slotted spoon and drain on kitchen paper. Serve as a starter with sweet chilli dipping sauce, lime wedges and crusty bread.

 Polenta Chilli Squid with Lime Mayo Half fill a deep saucepan with vegetable or groundnut oil and heat to 190°C (375°F), or until a cube of bread browns in 30 seconds. Meanwhile, place 8 tablespoons polenta (cornmeal), 1 teaspoon coarsely crushed black peppercorns, 1 teaspoon dried chilli flakes and 2 pinches of sea salt flakes in a large freezer bag. Add 625 g (1 lb 6 oz) ready-prepared squid rings to the bag and shake to coat in the mixture. Deep-fry in batches in the hot oil for 2–3 minutes until crisp and golden. Remove with a slotted spoon and drain on kitchen paper. Serve with oven chips and mayonnaise mixed with a little lime rind.

MID-FISH-HAT

30 Ginger and Lime Mackerel with Roasted Veg

Serves 2

1 small fennel bulb, trimmed and sliced

250 g (8 oz) new potatoes, thickly sliced

2 tomatoes, cut into wedges

2 tablespoons olive oil

½ teaspoon fennel seeds

2 whole mackerel

1 tablespoon soy sauce

1 cm (½ inch) piece of fresh root ginger, peeled and grated

finely grated rind and juice of 1 lime

1 teaspoon clear honey

salt and pepper

lime wedges, to serve

- Spread the fennel, potatoes and tomatoes over a baking tray, drizzle over the oil, scatter with the fennel seeds and season. Place in a preheated oven, 200°C (400°F), Gas Mark 6, for 25 minutes, turning occasionally, until cooked and lightly charred.

- Meanwhile, slash the mackerel skin several times and season both sides, then place on a foil-lined grill rack, skin side up. Mix together the soy sauce, ginger, lime rind and juice and honey in a small bowl and drizzle half of it over the fish.

- Cook under a preheated hot grill until the skin starts to crisp. Turn the fish over, drizzle over the remaining soy mixture and grill for a further 2–3 minutes until the mackerel is cooked through and flakes easily. Serve with the roasted vegetables and lime wedges.

---

1 Pan-Fried Ginger and Lime Mackerel with Roasted Veg Couscous Place a 100 g (3½ oz) pack roasted vegetable couscous in a heatproof bowl and just cover with boiling water. Cover with clingfilm and leave to stand for 5–8 minutes. Meanwhile, heat 1 tablespoon olive oil in a frying pan. Lightly dust 2 mackerel fillets in flour, then add to the pan, skin side down, and cook for 2 minutes until the skin is crisp. Turn the fish over and cook for a further 2–3 minutes until the mackerel is cooked through. Add 4 tablespoons ready-made chilli, coriander and ginger salad dressing and the juice of ½ lime to the pan, heat through and spoon over the fish to coat. Fluff up the couscous with a fork and serve with the mackerel fillets, pan juices and lime wedges.

2 Ginger and Lime Mackerel with Fennel Salad and New Potatoes Cook 250 g (8 oz) new potatoes in a saucepan of lightly salted boiling water for 15 minutes until tender. Thinly slice ½ trimmed fennel bulb and 4 radishes. Mix together in a bowl and drizzle over a little white wine vinegar and olive oil. Set aside. Meanwhile, prepare and grill the Ginger and Lime Mackerel as above. Drain the potatoes and lightly crush with a potato masher, then drizzle with a little olive oil and season. Serve the mackerel with the potatoes and fennel salad.

MID-FISH-DIJ

30 Baked Anchovy Tomatoes with Spaghetti

Serves 4

8 ripe tomatoes, quartered

8 anchovy fillets in oil, drained and chopped

2 garlic cloves, crushed

250 g (8 oz) feta cheese, crumbled

2 small handfuls of basil leaves, plus extra to garnish

4 tablespoons olive oil

4 slices of ciabatta bread, torn into pieces

250 g (8 oz) spaghetti

salt and pepper

- Scatter the tomatoes, anchovies, garlic, feta and basil over a large baking tray. Drizzle over half the oil and season with pepper (the anchovies are salty so there's no need to add salt). Bake in a preheated oven, 190°C (375°F), Gas Mark 5, for 20 minutes, turning occasionally, until the tomatoes are soft.

- Scatter the bread over a separate baking tray and drizzle with the remaining oil. Bake in the oven for the final 10 minutes of the baking time for the tomatoes.

- Meanwhile, cook the spaghetti in a large saucepan of lightly salted boiling water for 10 minutes, or until just tender, then drain and return to the pan. Lightly crush the tomato mixture with a fork, add the bread and toss with the spaghetti. Serve scattered with a few extra basil leaves.

 10 Anchovy Tomato Toasts

Heat 2 tablespoons olive oil in a flameproof frying pan, add 8 thickly sliced tomatoes, 2 crushed garlic cloves and 8 drained anchovy fillets in oil, chopped, and fry for 2–3 minutes, turning occasionally, until the tomatoes are soft. Scatter over 2 small handfuls of basil leaves, a drizzle of balsamic vinegar and 250 g (8 oz) chopped mozzarella cheese. Season with pepper and place the pan under a preheated medium grill for 2–3 minutes until the cheese is melted and bubbling. Serve spooned over toasted ciabatta bread.

 20 Spaghetti Puttanesca

Heat 4 tablespoons olive oil in a large frying pan, add 2 crushed garlic cloves and 8–12 roughly chopped ripe tomatoes and cook for 2 minutes, stirring. Add 4 drained anchovy fillets in oil, chopped, 1 teaspoon dried chilli flakes, 4 teaspoons drained capers and 2 tablespoons tomato purée. Simmer, stirring, for 5 minutes, adding a little water if the sauce is too thick. Season with pepper. Cook 250 g (8 oz) spaghetti in a large saucepan of lightly salted boiling water for 10 minutes, or until just tender. Drain and toss with the sauce, adding about 16 pitted black olives.

20 Smoked Haddock Rarebit

Serves 2

25 g (1 oz) butter
25 g (1 oz) plain flour
150 ml (¼ pint) milk
50 ml (2 fl oz) beer
½ teaspoon English mustard
1 teaspoon Worcestershire sauce
2 tablespoons grated Parmesan
  cheese
2 pieces of smoked haddock fillet,
  about 175 g (6 oz) each
1 tomato, sliced
125 g (4 oz) spinach leaves, rinsed
salt and pepper

- Melt the butter in a saucepan, add the flour and cook for 1 minute, stirring. Remove from the heat and gradually add the milk and beer. Return to the heat and bring to the boil, stirring continuously until thickened. Add the mustard, Worcestershire sauce and two-thirds of the cheese. Stir well and season.

- Place the fish in a buttered baking dish, spoon over the cheese sauce and place the tomato slices on top. Sprinkle with the remaining cheese and bake in a preheated oven, 200°C (400°F), Gas Mark 6, for 12–15 minutes until golden and the fish is cooked through.

- Towards the end of the cooking time, place the spinach in a saucepan without any extra water. Cover and cook for 2 minutes until just wilted, then drain. Serve with the rarebit.

---

10 Quick Hot-Smoked Haddock Rarebits

Heat 175 g (6 oz) shop-bought fresh cheese sauce, a dash of Worcestershire sauce and 2 tablespoons beer in a small saucepan. Stir in 200 g (7 oz) hot-smoked haddock or 125 g (4 oz) smoked mackerel, skinned and flaked, and heat through. Toast 4 thick slices of wholemeal bread on both sides, place on a foil-lined grill rack and spoon over the fish mixture and 50 g (2 oz) grated Cheddar cheese. Add 4 tomato halves to the grill rack. Cook under a preheated medium grill for 2–3 minutes until bubbling.

30 Smoked Haddock Rarebit Tart

Place 250 g (8 oz) smoked haddock fillet in a shallow pan. Pour over 150 ml (¼ pint) milk and bring to the boil, then reduce the heat and simmer for 3–4 minutes until cooked through. Remove the fish from the pan and reserve the milk. Melt 25 g (1 oz) butter in a saucepan, add 25 g (1 oz) plain flour and cook for 1 minute. Remove from the heat and gradually add the reserved milk and 50 ml (2 fl oz) beer. Return to the heat and bring to the boil, stirring until thickened. Stir in ½ teaspoon English mustard, 1 teaspoon Worcestershire sauce and 50 g (2 oz) grated Cheddar cheese and season. Flake the fish, discarding the skin, and stir into the sauce. Place ½ x 375 g (12 oz) sheet of ready-rolled puff pastry on a baking sheet. Spread the fish mixture over the pastry, leaving a 1 cm (½ inch) border around the edge. Top with 1 sliced tomato and sprinkle over 50 g (2 oz) grated Cheddar cheese. Bake in a preheated oven, 200°C (400°F), Gas Mark 6, for 15 minutes until golden and the pastry is crisp. Serve warm with salad.

 # Teriyaki Salmon with Egg Noodles

Serves 2

1 garlic clove, crushed

2 teaspoons sesame oil

3 tablespoons teriyaki sauce

2 pieces of salmon fillet, about
150 g (5 oz) each, with skin on

1 tablespoon vegetable oil

150 g (5 oz) medium egg noodles

75 g (3 oz) frozen soya beans or
peas

1 tablespoon sweet sherry

1 tablespoon soy sauce

1 teaspoon toasted sesame seeds

To garnish

2 spring onions, cut into thin strips

1 tablespoon chopped coriander
leaves

- Mix together the garlic, 1 teaspoon of the sesame oil and the teriyaki sauce in a shallow dish. Add the salmon and turn to coat in the sauce.

- Heat the vegetable oil in a frying pan, add the salmon and cook, skin side down, for 3–4 minutes until crisp, then turn the fish over and cook for a further 8–10 minutes until cooked through.

- Meanwhile, cook the noodles and soya beans or peas in a saucepan of lightly salted boiling water for 3 minutes until tender. Drain and return to the pan. Add the remaining sesame oil, the sherry and soy sauce and toss to coat.

- Pour any remaining teriyaki marinade into the salmon pan and heat through. Sprinkle with the sesame seeds and serve with the noodles, topped with the spring onions and coriander.

 ### Teriyaki Salmon Stir-Fry

Toss 300 g (10 oz) skinless salmon fillet, cut into chunks, in 2 tablespoons teriyaki sauce. Heat 1 tablespoon vegetable oil in a wok, add the salmon and cook, gently stirring occasionally, for about 5 minutes, or until cooked through. Add 1 tablespoon soy sauce and a squeeze of lime juice. Meanwhile, soak 150 g (5 oz) thread rice noodles in boiling water for 3 minutes. Drain and return to the pan. Add 2 thinly sliced spring onions and 1 tablespoon chopped coriander and toss to mix. Serve the fish with the noodles.

 ### Teriyaki Salmon with Sesame

Broccoli Mix together 1 crushed garlic clove, 1 teaspoon sesame oil and 3 tablespoons teriyaki sauce in a shallow dish. Add 2 pieces of salmon fillet, about 150 g (5 oz) each, turn to coat in the sauce and leave to marinate for 10 minutes. Heat 1 tablespoon vegetable oil in a frying pan, add the salmon and fry for 10–15 minutes, turning occasionally, until cooked through. Pour in any remaining teriyaki sauce and heat through. Meanwhile, heat 1 teaspoon sesame oil and 1 tablespoon vegetable oil in a

wok or frying pan, add 1 crushed garlic clove and 1 teaspoon peeled and grated fresh root ginger and cook for 1 minute. Add 200 g (7 oz) Tenderstem broccoli and stir-fry for 2 minutes. Pour in a little boiling water, cover and steam for 5 minutes until just tender. Add 1 tablespoon soy sauce and a squeeze of lime juice, then sprinkle with sesame seeds. Serve the salmon and broccoli with rice or noodles.

30 Thai Crab Cakes with Carrot Noodle Salad

Serves 2

½ red chilli, deseeded

2 spring onions

1 tablespoon coriander leaves

1 tablespoon Thai red curry paste

1 teaspoon Thai fish sauce

200 g (7 oz) skinless white fish fillets

170 g (6 oz) can crab meat, drained

1 small egg

150 g (5 oz) thread rice noodles

50 g (2 oz) sugar snap peas, halved lengthways

1 carrot, coarsely grated

2 tablespoons vegetable oil

lime wedges, to serve

For the dipping sauce

3 tablespoons light soy sauce

juice of ½ lime

1 teaspoon Thai fish sauce

pinch of caster sugar

½ red chilli, thinly sliced

- Place the chilli, spring onions and coriander in a food processor and pulse until chopped. Add the curry paste and fish sauce, then pulse again to mix. Add the fish, crab meat and egg and pulse until the mixture is well mixed but not smooth. Using wet hands, shape the mixture into 8 crab cakes. Cover and chill in the refrigerator for 10 minutes.

- Meanwhile, mix together the dipping sauce ingredients and set aside. Soak the noodles in boiling water for a few minutes to soften. Drain and rinse under cold water, then drain again and place in a bowl. Add the sugar snap peas, carrot and a little of the dipping sauce and mix well.

- Heat the vegetable oil in a frying pan, add the crab cakes and cook for 5 minutes, turning once, until golden and cooked through. Drain on kitchen paper and serve with the noodle salad, dipping sauce and lime wedges.

 Thai Crab and Carrot Salad Soak 150 g (5 oz) thread rice noodles in boiling water for 3 minutes to soften. Drain and rinse in a sieve, then place in a bowl. Add 170 g (6 oz) drained canned crab meat, 50 g (2 oz) sugar snap peas, 1 grated carrot and 4 tablespoons chopped coriander. Mix together 1 teaspoon Thai red curry paste, 1 teaspoon Thai fish sauce, the juice of ½ lime and 1 teaspoon soy sauce. Toss through the salad to mix.

 Quick Thai Crab Cakes with Carrot Salad Place 250 g (8 oz) skinless white fish fillets, such as cod, haddock or coley, a drained 170 g (6 oz) can crab meat, 1 tablespoon Thai red curry paste, 1 tablespoon coriander leaves and 1 teaspoon Thai fish sauce in a food processor. Pulse until well mixed but not smooth. Using wet hands, shape the mixture into 8 cakes. Cover and chill for 5 minutes. Shred 175 g (6 oz) Chinese leaves and mix with 1 coarsely grated carrot and 1 sliced spring onion. Mix together 2 teaspoons rice wine vinegar, a pinch of sugar and 2 teaspoons sesame oil. Add to the salad and toss to coat. Heat 1 tablespoon vegetable oil in a frying pan, add the crab cakes and cook for 5 minutes, turning once, until golden and cooked through. Serve with the salad and sweet chilli dipping sauce.

30 Seafood Tagliatelle

Serves 4

2 tablespoons olive oil
1 onion, chopped
2 garlic cloves, crushed
400 g (13 oz) can chopped
  tomatoes
100 ml (3½ fl oz) dry white wine
2 pinches of caster sugar
250 g (8 oz) tagliatelle
2 x 230 g (7½ oz) packs seafood
  selection
salt and pepper
2 tablespoons chopped parsley,
  to garnish

- Heat the oil in a large frying pan, add the onion and garlic and cook over a low heat for 3 minutes until slightly softened. Add the tomatoes, wine and sugar and season. Bring to the boil, then reduce the heat and simmer gently for 15–20 minutes, stirring occasionally and adding a little water if the sauce is too thick.

- Meanwhile, cook the tagliatelle in a large saucepan of lightly salted boiling water for about 8 minutes, or until just tender.

- Stir the seafood into the sauce and heat through for 2 minutes until piping hot. Drain the tagliatelle, then add to the seafood sauce and toss to coat. Serve sprinkled with the parsley.

 ### Creamy Seafood Pasta

Cook 500 g (1 lb) fresh egg tagliatelle in a large saucepan of lightly salted boiling water for 3 minutes, or until just tender. Meanwhile, heat 200 ml (7 fl oz) double cream, 100 ml (3½ fl oz) dry white wine, 2 crushed garlic cloves and 2 tablespoons chopped dill in a large saucepan. Add 2 x 230 g (7½ oz) packs seafood selection and heat through for 2–3 minutes until piping hot, then season. Drain the pasta, add to the sauce and toss to coat. Serve sprinkled with extra dill.

 ### Simple Seafood Risotto

Cook 2 x 250 g (8 oz) packs quick-cook saffron risotto rice according to the packet instructions, adding 50 g (2 oz) butter to the pan with the water. Add 150 g (5 oz) frozen peas for the final 3 minutes. Stir in 2 x 230 g (7½ oz) packs seafood selection, 2 tablespoons shredded basil leaves and 50 g (2 oz) grated Parmesan cheese and gently heat through for 3 minutes until piping hot. Serve with a sprinkling of Parmesan and black pepper.

MID-FISH-TEN

30 Asparagus, Lemon and Herb-Stuffed Salmon

Serves 4

20 fine asparagus spears, trimmed
butter, for greasing
8 pieces of salmon fillet, about 125 g (4 oz) each, skinned
finely grated rind and juice of 1 lemon
4 tablespoons chopped parsley
2 tablespoons chopped dill
salt and pepper

To serve

new potatoes
salad (optional)

- Cook the asparagus in a large saucepan of lightly salted boiling water for 3–4 minutes until just tender. Drain well.

- Lightly grease a baking sheet, then place 4 salmon fillets on the sheet, skinned side up. Toss the asparagus with the lemon rind, parsley and dill and season well. Arrange on top of the salmon fillets, then top with the remaining salmon fillets, skinned side down. Using 3 pieces of kitchen string on each, roughly tie the salmon pieces together to enclose the filling. Season and pour over the lemon juice.

- Place in a preheated oven, 220°C (425°F), Gas Mark 7, for 10 minutes, or until the fish is opaque and cooked through. Serve with new potatoes and salad, if liked.

---

10 Grilled Lemon Salmon with Asparagus

Asparagus Place 4 salmon fillets, about 125 g (4 oz) each, on a foil-lined grill rack and season well with pepper. Finely grate 2 lemons, sprinkle the rind over the top of each and press into the fish, then squeeze over the juice from the lemons. Cook under a preheated hot grill for 4–5 minutes, or until opaque and cooked through. Meanwhile, heat 4 tablespoons olive oil in a large saucepan, add 300 g (10 oz) trimmed asparagus spears and cook over a high heat for 5 minutes, stirring and tossing until tender. Serve with the grilled salmon.

20 Lemony Salmon and Asparagus

Cook 2 bunches of trimmed and roughly chopped asparagus spears in a large saucepan of lightly salted boiling water for 2 minutes, then immediately drain and rinse under cold running water. Set aside. Heat 4 tablespoons olive oil in a large wok or frying pan, add 600 g (1 lb 5 oz) cubed skinless salmon fillet and cook for 5–6 minutes, turning frequently without breaking up the pieces, until golden all over and cooked through. Place the finely grated rind and juice of 2 lemons in a bowl, stir in 400 ml (14 fl oz) crème fraîche and season well.

Spoon into the pan, add the drained asparagus and heat through for 2 minutes until the sauce is piping hot. Serve hot.

30 Prawn Jambalaya

Serves 4

2 tablespoons olive oil
1 large green pepper, cored, deseeded and thinly sliced
4 celery sticks, thinly sliced
350 g (11½ oz) cooked peeled king prawns
2 tablespoons Cajun seasoning
2 x 400 g (13 oz) cans kidney beans, rinsed and drained
4 large fresh tomatoes, roughly chopped
300 ml (½ pint) hot fish stock
100 g (3½ oz) coconut cream, roughly chopped
250 g (8 oz) easy cook basmati rice
salt and pepper
thyme, to garnish

- Heat the oil in a large frying pan, add the green peppers and celery and cook over a medium heat for 7–8 minutes until starting to soften. Add the prawns and Cajun seasoning and fry, stirring, for 5 minutes.

- Add the kidney beans, tomatoes, stock and coconut cream and bring to the boil, then reduce the heat, cover and simmer for 10 minutes, stirring occasionally, until piping hot.

- Meanwhile, cook the rice in a large saucepan of lightly salted boiling water for 15–20 minutes until tender. Drain well, then add to the prawn mixture and cook for a further 2 minutes, stirring occasionally, until piping hot. Season well and serve garnished with thyme.

 ### 10 Cajun-Spiced Prawns

Heat 2 tablespoons olive oil in a large frying pan, add 1 thinly sliced onion and cook for 3 minutes, then add 500 g (1 lb) cooked peeled king prawns and cook over a high heat for 2 minutes, then add 2 teaspoons Cajun seasoning and 4 roughly chopped tomatoes and cook for a further 2–3 minutes until piping hot. Add 125 ml (4 fl oz) coconut milk and heat for a few seconds, then stir in 4 tablespoons chopped coriander leaves. Serve with ready-cooked rice.

 ### 20 Cajun Prawn Rice and Peas

Place 250 g (8 oz) easy cook basmati rice, 600 ml (1 pint) hot chicken stock and a 400 ml (14 fl oz) can coconut milk in a large saucepan and bring to the boil. Reduce the heat, cover and simmer for 12–15 minutes until the rice is tender, adding a little more water if necessary. Meanwhile, heat 2 tablespoons olive oil in a large frying pan, add 2 onions, cut into slim wedges, and cook for 5 minutes until golden and softened, then add 350 g (11½ oz) cooked peeled prawns and 4 teaspoons Cajun seasoning and cook over a high heat for 3–4 minutes until the prawns and onions are sizzling. Add a 400 g (13 oz) can kidney beans, rinsed and drained, to the rice and stir through, then add the prawns and onions and toss to mix. Serve scattered with chopped coriander leaves.

30 Smoked Fish and Fennel Pie

Serves 2

25 g (1 oz) butter
1 onion, finely sliced
1 small or ½ fennel bulb, trimmed and finely sliced
375 g (12 oz) skinless smoked haddock fillet, cubed
125 g (4 oz) smoked salmon trimmings
200 ml (7 fl oz) half-fat crème fraîche
juice of ½ lemon
2 tablespoons water
425 g (14 oz) tub fresh ready-cooked mashed potatoes
6 tablespoons chopped parsley
2 tablespoons chopped dill
25 g (1 oz) finely grated smoked Cheddar cheese

- Heat the butter in a saucepan, add the onion and fennel and cook over a medium heat for 5 minutes until softened. Transfer to a bowl, add the smoked fish, crème fraîche and lemon juice and toss together, adding the measurement water to loosen.

- Spoon into 2 individual gratin dishes. Place the mash in a bowl, add the herbs and mix well. Spoon over the fish, then scatter with the cheese. Place in a preheated oven, 220°C (425°F), Gas Mark 7, for 15–20 minutes until heated through.

- Place the dishes under a preheated hot grill for 1 minute until golden.

---

10 Smoked Fish and Fennel Pan-Fry

Heat 25 g (1 oz) butter in a frying pan, add 1 small finely sliced onion and ½ trimmed and finely sliced fennel bulb and cook for 3–4 minutes until softened. Stir in 200 ml (7 fl oz) half-fat crème fraîche and the juice of ½ lemon and heat for 1 minute. Add 250 g (8 oz) cubed skinless smoked haddock fillet, 125 g (4 oz) smoked salmon trimmings and 1 tablespoon chopped dill. Bring to the boil, then reduce the heat, cover and simmer for 3–4 minutes until the fish is cooked through.

20 Smoked Fish and Fennel Crêpes

Heat 25 g (1 oz) butter in a frying pan, add 1 small finely sliced onion and ½ small trimmed and finely sliced fennel bulb and cook for 3–4 minutes until softened. Remove from the heat and add 375 g (12 oz) cubed skinless smoked haddock fillet, 125 g (4 oz) smoked salmon trimmings and 6 tablespoons water. Return to the heat and bring to the boil, then reduce the heat, cover and simmer for 3 minutes until the fish is opaque and cooked through. Spoon in 200 ml (7 fl oz) half-fat crème fraîche and the juice of ½ lemon and heat for a further 1 minute. Stir in 1 tablespoon chopped dill. Spoon the mixture on to 4 ready-made pancakes, then roll up to enclose the filling, place in a lightly greased shallow gratin dish and scatter with 50 g (2 oz) grated Cheddar cheese. Cook under a preheated hot grill for 3–4 minutes until golden and bubbling.

Chilled Coconut Soup with Sizzling Prawns

Serves 2

400 ml (14 fl oz) can coconut milk, chilled

150 ml (¼ pint) chilled natural yogurt

¼ cucumber, finely chopped

3 tablespoons finely chopped mint leaves

pepper

1 tablespoon chopped coriander leaves, to garnish (optional)

naan bread, to serve

For the prawns

1 tablespoon sunflower oil

175 g (6 oz) cooked peeled king prawns

1 teaspoon ready-minced garlic

½ teaspoon cayenne pepper

- Place the coconut milk, yogurt, cucumber and mint into a large jug and mix well, then season with plenty of pepper. Pour into 2 serving bowls.

- Heat the oil in a frying pan until smoking. Toss the prawns with the garlic and cayenne pepper, then carefully tip into the hot oil and cook over a high heat for 2–3 minutes until golden in places and sizzling.

- Divide the prawns between the serving bowls, sprinkle with coriander, if liked, and serve immediately with naan bread.

 Prawn and Coconut Pan-Fry

Heat 1 tablespoon sunflower oil in a large frying pan, add 1 onion, 250 g (8 oz) sliced courgettes and 1 cored, deseeded and roughly chopped red pepper and stir-fry for 5 minutes. Add 250 g (8 oz) cooked peeled king prawns, 4 tablespoons roughly chopped coriander leaves and ½ teaspoon each of cayenne pepper, ground coriander and ground cumin and fry, stirring, for a further 2 minutes. Add 150 ml (¼ pint) coconut milk, bring to the boil and serve immediately with rice.

 Prawn and Coconut Curry

Heat 1 tablespoon sunflower oil in a saucepan, add 1 thinly sliced onion and 1 thinly sliced garlic clove and cook for 3 minutes. Add 4 tablespoons roughly chopped coriander leaves and stalks and ½ teaspoon each of cayenne pepper, ground coriander and ground cumin and cook for a few seconds. Pour in a 400 ml (14 fl oz) can coconut milk and bring to the boil, then reduce the heat, cover and simmer for 10 minutes. Add 250 g (8 oz) cooked peeled king prawns and cook for a further 5 minutes until piping hot. Blend 1 teaspoon cornflour with 1 tablespoon water, then add to the pan and stir well until slightly thickened. Serve with rice.

Pan-Fried Herby Salmon with Creamy Mascarpone Sauce

Serves 2

2 pieces of salmon fillet, about
175 g (6 oz) each, with skin on
1 garlic clove, crushed
5 tablespoons chopped parsley,
dill and tarragon
1 tablespoon olive oil
15 g (½ oz) unsalted butter
4 tablespoons crème fraîche
3 tablespoons mascarpone
cheese
salt and pepper

- Place the salmon fillets in a bowl with the garlic and 3 tablespoons of the herbs and gently turn to heavily coat in the mixture. Season well.

- Heat the oil and butter in a frying pan, add the salmon and cook over a medium-high heat for 3 minutes on each side until golden and cooked through. Reduce the heat to a gentle simmer and turn the fillets on to the skin side.

- Mix together the crème fraîche, mascarpone and remaining herbs. Spoon into the pan and cook gently for 2–3 minutes, gently stirring around the fish until the sauce is piping hot but not boiling.

- Serve the fish on 2 warm serving plates with the sauce spooned over.

 Creamy Salmon with Herbs

Heat 1 tablespoon olive oil in a frying pan, add 300 g (10 oz) cubed skinless salmon fillet and cook for 4–5 minutes until cooked through. Add the finely grated rind and juice of 1 lemon, 5 tablespoons crème fraîche and 3 tablespoons mascarpone cheese and heat gently for a further 2 minutes. Stir in 3 tablespoons chopped parsley and dill and serve.

Creamy Salmon Pie with Herby Mash

Place 2 salmon fillets, about 125 g (4 oz) each, on a foil-lined grill rack and cook under a preheated hot grill for 5 minutes, or until opaque and cooked through. Meanwhile, melt 25 g (1 oz) butter in a saucepan, add 25 g (1 oz) plain flour and cook for a few seconds. Remove from the heat and gradually add 300 ml (½ pint) milk. Return to the heat and bring to the boil, stirring continuously until boiled and thickened. Add the finely grated rind and juice of 1 lemon, then flake the fish, discarding the skin, and fold in with 125 g (4 oz) cooked peeled prawns. Spoon the mixture into a shallow gratin dish. Mix together a 500 g (1 lb) pack fresh ready-cooked mashed potatoes, 4 tablespoons chopped parsley and dill and 3 tablespoons mascarpone cheese in a bowl, then spoon over the fish mixture. Cook under a preheated medium grill for 5–10 minutes until piping hot.

30 Baked Herby Cod with Gruyère and Spinach Mash

Serves 4

4 pieces of skinless cod fillet or
loin, about 200 g (7 oz) each
juice of 1 lemon
2 tablespoons olive oil
4 tablespoons chopped flat leaf
parsley
4 slices of prosciutto

For the mash

1 kg (2 lb) potatoes, peeled and
cubed
50 g (2 oz) butter
4 tablespoons crème fraîche
100 g (3½ oz) finely grated
Gruyère cheese
40 g (1½ oz) baby spinach leaves
salt and pepper

- Place the cod, lemon juice, oil and parsley in a large non-metallic bowl and gently toss to lightly coat. Season with pepper. Tightly wrap each piece of fish with 1 slice of prosciutto and place on a large baking sheet. Place in a preheated oven, 220 °C (425 °F), Gas Mark 7, for 12–15 minutes, or until cooked through.

- Meanwhile, make the mash. Cook the potatoes in a large saucepan of lightly salted boiling water for 15 minutes until tender. Drain, then return to the pan and mash with the butter and crème fraîche. Fold in the cheese and spinach until the cheese is melted and the spinach wilted, then season. Spoon on to 4 warm serving plates and top with the fish.

---

10 Pan-Fried Cod with Herby Cheese Mash

Heat 2 tablespoons olive oil in a large frying pan, add 8 torn slices of prosciutto and cook over a high heat for 2 minutes until crisp. Remove from the pan. Heat 25 g (1 oz) butter in the pan, add 4 cod loins, and cook for 3 minutes on each side, or until cooked through. Mix together 600 g (1 lb 5 oz) fresh ready-cooked mashed potatoes, 50 g (2 oz) grated Gruyère cheese and 2 tablespoons chopped parsley in a microwaveable bowl and heat in a microwave for 2 minutes. Serve the cod on the mash, scattered with the prosciutto.

20 Herby Cod with Cheesy Spinach and Mash Pots

Place 4 cod loins, about 150 g (5 oz) each, in a large roasting tin and season well. Scatter with 4 tablespoons chopped parsley. Roast in a preheated oven, 220 °C (425 °F), Gas Mark 7, for 15–20 minutes, or until cooked through. Meanwhile, mix together 600 g (1 lb 5 oz) fresh ready-cooked mashed potatoes and 100 g (3½ oz) spinach leaves in a bowl. Spoon into 4 ramekins and press down firmly. Sprinkle with 100 g (3½ oz) grated Gruyère cheese. Place at the top of the oven for

10–15 minutes until heated through. Serve with the fish.

20 Thai Green Fish Curry with Lime Leaves

Serves 4

2 tablespoons vegetable oil

1 large red pepper, cored, deseeded and cut into chunks

250 g (8 oz) mangetout

1 bunch of spring onions, roughly chopped

2 lemon grass stalks, finely chopped

4 lime leaves, finely shredded

1 x 400 ml (14 fl oz) can reduced fat coconut milk

3–4 tablespoons Thai green curry paste

350 g (11½ oz) skinless white fish fillets, such as cod or haddock, cubed

150 g (5 oz) cooked peeled prawns

8 tablespoons chopped coriander leaves

Thai sticky rice, to serve (optional)

• Heat the oil in a large saucepan, add the red pepper and cook for 4 minutes, then add the mangetout, spring onions, lemon grass and lime leaves and cook over a medium heat for a further 3–4 minutes until softened.

• Pour in the coconut milk and curry paste and stir well, then simmer gently for 3 minutes. Add the fish and prawns and continue to cook for 5 minutes until the fish is opaque and cooked through.

• Stir in the coriander. Then spoon into 4 warm serving bowls and serve with Thai sticky rice, if liked.

---

10 Thai Prawn Stir-Fry

Heat 2 tablespoons vegetable oil in a large wok, add 2 cored, deseeded and thinly sliced red peppers and 250 g (8 oz) mangetout and stir-fry for 2 minutes. Add 350 g (11½ oz) cooked peeled prawns, 2 teaspoons minced lemon grass and 2 teaspoons Thai green curry paste and stir-fry for 2 minutes, then add 250 g (8 oz) bean sprouts and cook for 1 minute. Add 125 ml (4 fl oz) coconut milk and heat through until piping hot. Serve with ready-cooked rice, if liked.

30 Thai-Style Fishcakes

Cook 175 g (6 oz) Thai sticky rice in a large saucepan of lightly salted boiling water for 15 minutes until tender and cooked. Drain well. Meanwhile, place 1 cored, deseeded and finely chopped red pepper, 75 g (3 oz) finely chopped mangetout, 3 finely chopped spring onions, ½ finely chopped lemon grass stalk, 1 finely chopped lime leaf and 1½ teaspoons Thai green curry paste in a large bowl. Add 275 g (9 oz) finely chopped skinless white fish fillet, such as cod or haddock, 125 g (4 oz) roughly chopped cooked peeled prawns, 6 tablespoons chopped coriander leaves, the drained rice and 2 small eggs and mix together well. Shape the mixture into 8 small patties. Heat 2 tablespoons vegetable oil in a large frying pan, add the patties and cook over a high heat for 2 minutes on each side until heated through, golden and a light crust is formed. Serve with a simple salad.

30 Chilli Seafood Stew

Serves 2

2 tablespoons olive oil

1 red onion, cut into slim wedges

1 small red chilli, deseeded and thinly sliced

1 garlic clove, sliced

250 g (8 oz) potatoes, peeled and cubed

200 g (7 oz) ready-prepared squid rings

400 g (13 oz) can chopped tomatoes

150 ml (¼ pint) white wine

3 tablespoons sun-dried tomato paste

2 tablespoons sun-blush tomatoes in oil, drained

2 tablespoons thyme leaves

250 g (8 oz) live mussels

175 g (6 oz) red mullet fillets, skinned and cut into chunks

warm crusty bread, to serve

- Heat the oil in a large frying pan, add the onion, chilli and garlic and cook over a medium heat for 5–8 minutes until pale golden and softened. Add the potatoes and squid rings and cook for a further 2 minutes.

- Add 150 ml (¼ pint) water, the chopped tomatoes, wine and tomato paste to the pan and stir well, then add the sun-blush tomatoes and thyme and cook for 8 minutes.

- Meanwhile, wash the mussels under cold running water and discard any that don't shut when tapped. Pull off any fibrous 'beards' and remove any barnacles, then rinse again.

- Add the red mullet to the pan and stir gently through, then add the mussels, cover and bring to the boil. Cook for 5–7 minutes, shaking the pan occasionally until the fish is cooked through and the mussels have opened. Discard any that remain closed. Serve with warm crusty bread to mop up the juices.

 Seafood, Chilli and Tomato Pan-Fry

Heat 1 tablespoon olive oil in a frying pan, add 1 small roughly chopped onion and cook for 2 minutes. Add a 400 g (13 oz) can chopped tomatoes, ½ teaspoon dried chilli flakes, 150 ml (¼ pint) white wine and a 300 g (10 oz) pack seafood selection and bring to the boil. Reduce the heat, cover and simmer for 5 minutes until piping hot. Serve with crusty bread.

 Spicy Seafood Soup

Heat 2 tablespoons olive oil in a large saucepan, add 1 thinly sliced red onion, ½ small deseeded and thinly sliced red chilli and 1 sliced garlic clove and cook for 3–4 minutes until softened. Add 200 g (7 oz) ready-prepared squid rings, a 400 g (13 oz) can chopped tomatoes, 150 ml (¼ pint) white wine, 2 tablespoons sun-dried tomato paste and 300 ml (½ pint) hot fish stock and bring to the boil. Reduce the heat, cover and simmer for 5 minutes. Meanwhile, wash 250 g (8 oz) live mussels under cold running water and discard any that don't shut when tapped. Pull off any fibrous 'beards' and remove any barnacles, then rinse again. Add to the pan and stir well, then cover and cook for 5–7 minutes until the mussels have opened, discarding any that remain closed. Scatter with thyme leaves and serve.

MID-FISH-VAO

Chilli and Lemon Fishcakes

Serves 2

375 g (12 oz) potatoes, peeled and cut into small chunks
250 g (8 oz) cod loins
8 tablespoons water
2 tablespoons olive oil
8 spring onions, roughly chopped
½ red chilli, deseeded and roughly chopped
finely grated rind of 1 lemon
3 tablespoons chopped parsley
1 egg, beaten
125 g (4 oz) ciabatta breadcrumbs
6 tablespoons vegetable oil
salt and pepper

To serve

lemon wedges
tartare sauce

- Cook the potatoes in a large saucepan of lightly salted boiling water for 10 minutes until tender. Drain the potatoes, then return to the pan and mash with a potato masher.

- Meanwhile, place the cod in a small saucepan with the measurement water and season well. Bring to the boil, then reduce the heat, cover and simmer for 5 minutes until opaque and cooked through. Drain well, then flake.

- Heat the olive oil in a large frying pan, add the spring onions and chilli and cook over a high heat for 2 minutes. Add to the potato mixture. Then add the flaked fish, lemon rind and parsley and fold through. Shape the mixture into 4 patties.

- Place the beaten egg in a bowl and the breadcrumbs in another. Coat the patties in the egg, then in the breadcrumbs.

- Heat the vegetable oil in a large frying pan, add the fishcakes and cook over a high heat for 5–6 minutes, turning, until golden and cooked through. Serve with lemon wedges and tartare sauce.

Chilli and Lemon Tuna Balls

Mix together a 300 g (10 oz) pack fresh ready-cooked mashed potatoes and a 200 g (7 oz) can tuna, drained, in a bowl. Heat 1 tablespoon olive oil in a frying pan, add 4 chopped spring onions and ½ deseeded and chopped red chilli and cook for 2 minutes. Fold into the potato mixture with the grated rind of 1 lemon, then shape into 4 rough balls. Heat a further 2 tablespoons olive oil in a small frying pan, add the tuna balls and cook over a high heat for 3–4 minutes, turning, until hot.

Deep-Fried Chilli Cod Balls

Cook 375 g (12 oz) peeled and chopped potatoes in a large saucepan of lightly salted boiling water for 10 minutes until tender. Drain and mash. Place 250 g (8 oz) cod loins and 8 tablespoons water in a small saucepan, cover tightly and cook for 5 minutes until cooked through. Heat 1 tablespoon olive oil in a small frying pan, add 6 finely chopped spring onions and ½ small deseeded and chopped red chilli and cook for 3 minutes. Flake the fish and add to the mash with the spring onions and chilli.

Add the finely grated rind of 1 small lemon. Shape into 8 small balls and roll in 125 g (4 oz) fine ciabatta breadcrumbs to coat. Half fill a deep saucepan with vegetable oil and heat to 190°C (375°F), or until a cube of bread browns in 30 seconds. Deep-fry the balls in the hot oil for 2–3 minutes until golden. Remove with a slotted spoon and drain on kitchen paper. Meanwhile, mix together 200 ml (7 fl oz) crème fraîche, the grated rind of 1 small lemon and 3 tablespoons chopped parsley in a small bowl. Serve the dip with the fish balls.

30 Roasted Garlicky Herb Sea Bass, Fennel and Potatoes

Serves 2

2 whole sea bass, about 300 g
(10 oz) each, gutted

1 garlic clove, sliced

4 tablespoons chopped parsley

2 tablespoons chopped thyme
leaves

1 lemon, halved and sliced

1 fennel bulb, trimmed and thinly
sliced

375 g (12 oz) potatoes, cut into
slim wedges

1 tablespoon olive oil

salt and pepper

- Place the fish in a roasting tin and slash both sides deep to the bone. Season well with pepper.

- Mix together the garlic and herbs in a bowl, then rub the mixture over the fish, pushing it into the slashes. Tuck the lemon slices and fennel under and on top of the fish. Toss the potatoes with the oil and season well, then arrange around the fish.

- Roast in a preheated oven, 200°C (400°F), Gas Mark 6, for 20–25 minutes, or until the potatoes are golden and the fish is cooked through.

 Sea Bass Fillets with Garlic and Herb Butter Heat 25 g (1 oz) butter in a frying pan, add 2 sea bass fillets, 75–125 g (3–4 oz) each, and cook over a medium heat for 2 minutes on each side until cooked through. Add 1 roughly chopped garlic clove and 1 tablespoon chopped thyme leaves and cook gently for a further 1 minute. Serve with microwaved baked potatoes with the herb butter spooned over.

 Pan-Fried Herb and Garlic Sea Bass and Fennel Slash 2 gutted sea bass, about 300 g (10 oz) each, several times on each side and season well. Heat 25 g (1 oz) butter in a large frying pan, add 1 small trimmed and thinly sliced fennel bulb and 1 thinly sliced garlic clove and cook over a medium heat for 3–4 minutes until slightly softened. Add the fish to the pan and cook for 4 minutes on each side, or until the flesh is opaque and cooked through. Scatter with 1 tablespoon chopped thyme leaves and season well. Serve with crusty bread.

10 Scallop, Bacon and Pine Nut Pan-Fry

Serves 4

25 g (1 oz) butter
300 g (10 oz) smoked streaky bacon, cut into pieces
350 g (11½ oz) scallops, halved widthways if large
4 tablespoons pine nuts
8 tablespoons chopped parsley
finely grated rind of 1 lemon
crusty bread, to serve

- Heat the butter in a large frying pan, add the bacon and cook over a high heat for 3 minutes until golden.

- Add the scallops and pine nuts and cook for 3–4 minutes until the scallops are cooked through and the pine nuts are golden. Stir in the parsley and lemon rind. Divide the mixture between 4 dishes, spoon over any juices and serve with plenty of crusty bread.

 Griddled Scallops in Bacon

Place 16 large scallops, 2 tablespoons chopped parsley and the finely grated rind of 1 lemon in a bowl and toss well to coat. Wrap 1 streaky bacon rasher around each scallop, then secure with cocktail sticks. Heat 25 g (1 oz) butter in a griddle pan, add the scallops and cook over a high heat for 2 minutes on each side until golden and cooked through. Serve with a simple salad and crusty bread.

 Creamy Baked Scallops and Bacon

Heat 25 g (1 oz) butter in a large frying pan, add 8 roughly chopped streaky bacon rashers and cook over a medium heat for 3–4 minutes until crisp. Add 16 scallops and fry for 2 minutes. Remove with a slotted spoon and set aside. Add 25 g (1 oz) plain flour to the pan and cook for a few seconds, stirring. Remove from the heat and gradually add 300 ml (½ pint) milk. Return to the heat and bring to the boil, stirring continuously until boiled and thickened. Return the scallops and bacon to the pan and fold into the sauce with 8 tablespoons chopped parsley. Spoon into 4 clean and empty scallop shells or ramekins and scatter with 8 tablespoons fresh breadcrumbs. Bake in a preheated oven, 190°C (375°F), Gas Mark 5, for 10 minutes until the breadcrumbs are golden. Serve with green beans, if liked.

MID-FISH-TED

30 Juicy Cod Burgers with Tartare Sauce

Serves 2

3 tablespoons plain flour

2 cod loins, about 200 g (7 oz) each

1 egg, beaten

75 g (3 oz) fresh wholemeal breadcrumbs

1 tablespoon finely chopped parsley

finely grated rind of ½ lemon

4 tablespoons sunflower oil

2 good-quality soft brown rolls

2 thick slices of large beef tomato

2 handfuls of watercress leaves

salt and pepper

For the tartare sauce

2 tablespoons crème fraîche

2 tablespoons mayonnaise

1 tablespoon drained and chopped capers

finely grated rind of ½ lemon

- Season the flour on a plate, then toss the cod loins in the seasoned flour. Place the beaten egg on a second plate, add the fish and gently coat. Toss the breadcrumbs with the parsley and lemon rind, then coat the fish in the breadcrumbs.

- Heat the oil in a large frying pan, add the coated fish and cook over a medium heat for 2–3 minutes on each side, or until golden and cooked through.

- Meanwhile, mix together all the tartare sauce ingredients in a small bowl.

- To assemble the burgers, cut the rolls in half. Place 1 tomato slice on each of the roll bases, add the hot fish loins and top with spoonfuls of the tartare sauce and the watercress. Top with the remaining bun halves and serve.

 Cod Rolls with Tartare Sauce

Heat 15 g (½ oz) butter in a frying pan, add 2 seasoned cod loins, about 125 g (4 oz) each, and cook for 2–3 minutes on each side, or until cooked through. Halve 2 soft rolls and place 1 slice of tomato in the base of each, then add the fish. Spoon 1 tablespoon of ready-made tartare sauce over the top of each. Top with watercress and the remaining bun halves.

 Fish Finger Rolls with Tartare Sauce

Mix together 2 tablespoons each of crème fraîche and mayonnaise, 1 tablespoon drained capers and the finely grated rind of 1 lemon in a small bowl. Season well with pepper. Cook 6 fish fingers under a preheated medium grill for 8 minutes, turning once, until golden and cooked through. Cut 2 good-quality soft rolls in half and place 1 large slice of tomato in the base of each, then add 3 fish fingers to each. Spoon on 2 tablespoons of the tartare sauce and place a handful of watercress leaves on top. Top with the remaining bun halves and serve.

MID-FISH-WEP

Oriental Prawn and Crab Stir-Fry

Serves 2

2 tablespoons sesame oil

2 teaspoons peeled and chopped fresh root ginger

300 g (10 oz) pack ready-prepared stir-fry vegetables

1 head of pak choi, halved and leaves separated

175 g (6 oz) cooked peeled king prawns

50 g (2 oz) mixed fresh white and dark crab meat

2 tablespoons soy sauce

4 tablespoons sweet chilli sauce

chopped coriander leaves, to garnish

- Heat the oil in a large wok or frying pan, add the ginger and cook for a few seconds. Add the vegetables and stir-fry for 4 minutes.

- Add the prawns and cook for 1 minute, then add the crab meat and cook and toss over a high heat for 2–3 minutes until piping hot. Add the soy sauce and chilli sauce and toss again to coat. Serve scattered with coriander.

 Gingered Prawn and Crab Rice

Cook 125 g (4 oz) easy cook rice in a saucepan of lightly salted boiling water for 10–12 minutes until tender, then drain. Meanwhile, heat 2 tablespoons sesame oil in a frying pan, add 2 teaspoons peeled and chopped fresh root ginger and 300 g (10 oz) ready-prepared stir-fry vegetables and stir-fry for 3–4 minutes. Add 175 g (6 oz) cooked peeled king prawns and 50 g (2 oz) mixed fresh white and dark crab meat and cook for 3 minutes until piping hot. Add the rice, 2 tablespoons soy sauce and 4 tablespoons sweet chilli sauce to the crab mixture. Toss and cook for 2 minutes until piping hot.

 Prawn and Crab Spring Rolls

Heat 2 tablespoons sesame oil in a large frying pan, add 200 g (7 oz) shop-bought ready-prepared stir-fry vegetables and cook for 2 minutes. Add 75 g (3 oz) cooked peeled prawns and continue to fry, stirring, for 2 minutes until piping hot, then add 50 g (2 oz) fresh crab meat. Remove from the heat and toss to mix. Add 3 tablespoons sweet chilli sauce and 2 tablespoons chopped coriander leaves and toss again. Place 1 sheet of filo pastry on a board and place a second sheet on top. Pile one-quarter of the crab mixture in the centre of the sheets, fold the sides over the filling, then fold in each end and roll up to form a spring roll. Repeat to make 4 spring rolls. Place on a baking sheet and bake in a preheated oven, 220°C (425°F), Gas Mark 7, for 12–15 minutes until crisp and golden.

Pan-Fried Prosciutto-Wrapped Salmon

Serves 2

2 skinless salmon fillets, about
175 g (6 oz) each
2 tablespoons chopped parsley
2 slices of prosciutto
1 tablespoon olive oil
salt and pepper

To serve

rocket salad
lemon wedges

- Season the salmon well, then scatter with the parsley. Tightly wrap each fillet with 1 slice of prosciutto.

- Heat the oil in a frying pan, add the salmon and cook over a medium-high heat for 7–8 minutes, turning occasionally, until golden and cooked through.

- Serve with a rocket salad and lemon wedges.

Grilled Salmon with Creamy Prosciutto Sauce Heat 1 tablespoon olive oil in a saucepan, add 4 slices of prosciutto, snipped into pieces, and cook for 3–4 minutes until crisp and golden. Remove with a slotted spoon and set aside. Add 1 tablespoon plain flour to the pan and cook for a few seconds, stirring. Remove from the heat and gradually add 300 ml (½ pint) milk. Add 50 g (2 oz) spinach leaves and ½ teaspoon ground nutmeg and season well with pepper. Return to the heat and bring to the boil, stirring continuously until boiled, thickened and the spinach has wilted. Stir in the reserved prosciutto, set aside and keep warm. Place 2 salmon fillets, about 175 g (6 oz) each, with skin on, on a foil-lined grill rack and season with pepper. Cook under a preheated hot grill for 2–3 minutes on each side, or until opaque and cooked through. Serve the salmon with the sauce spooned over.

Roasted Prosciutto-Wrapped Salmon and Potatoes Tightly wrap each of 2 skinless salmon fillets, about 175 g (6 oz) each, with 1 slice of prosciutto. Place in a lightly greased roasting tin. Add 300 g (10 oz) baby new potatoes and season well. Scatter with 2 tablespoons chopped parsley and roast in the top of a preheated oven, 200°C (400°F), Gas Mark 6, for 20 minutes, or until the fish is cooked through and the potatoes are golden and tender.

QuickCook
Vegetarian

Recipes listed by cooking time

30

Spinach and Feta
Filo Parcels   180

Pea, Leek and Potato
Soup with Pesto and
Cheesy Toasts   182

Curried Cauliflower,
Lentil and Rice Pot   184

Falafels with Beetroot Salad
and Mint Yogurt   186

Cheesy Courgette Bakes   188

Sweetcorn Rosti with
Chilli Salsa   190

Stuffed Pasta, Pine Nut
and Butternut Gratin   192

Roasted Butternut and
Red Pepper Soup   194

Garlic and Herb
Mushroom Tart   196

Tomato and Bean Soup   198

Tomato and Mozzarella
Sourdough Bake   200

Warm Chickpea, Artichoke
and Tomato Stew   202

Asparagus, Aubergine,
Brie and Tomato Quiche   204

Spinach and Feta
Burritos   206

Blue Cheese, Spinach and
Walnut Gnocchi Bake   208

Pea, Parmesan and
Mint Risotto   210

Goats' Cheese and Butternut
Squash Stuffed Peppers   212

Sweet Chilli and Tempura
Vegetable Noodles   214

Yellow Lentil Dahl   216

Pepper, Caper and
Spinach Penne Bake   218

Harissa Aubergine and
Chickpea Dip with
Flatbread Crisps   220

Roasted Carrot and Beetroot
Pearl Barley with Feta   222

Baked Spinach and
Leek Frittata   224

Mozzarella, Tomato and
Basil Thin-Crust Pizza   226

20

Spinach and Feta
Salad Tarts   180

Chunky Pea, Leek and
Pesto Soup   182

Easy Cauliflower and
Lentil Pilau   184

Chickpea Burgers with
Beetroot   186

Cheesy Courgette
Carbonara   188

Sweetcorn Fritters with
Sweet Chilli Dip   190

Creamy Squash, Pine Nuts
and Stuffed Pasta   192

Spiced Butternut
Squash Soup   194

Garlic, Herb and Brie
Stuffed Mushrooms   196

Mediterranean
Tomato Soup   198

Warm Tomato and
Mozzarella Salad with
Sourdough Croûtons   200

Chickpea, Artichoke and
Tomato Pan-Fry   202

Asparagus, Aubergine,
Brie and Tomato Tortilla   204

Warm Spinach and
Feta Tortilla Slices   206

10

Blue Cheese, Spinach and Walnut Tart   208

Cheesy Pea and Mint Rice Balls   210

Red Pepper, Butternut and Goats' Cheese Soup   212

Tempura Mixed Vegetables with Chilli Sauce   214

Red Lentil Dahl with Warm Naan   216

Pepper, Caper and Spinach Pappardelle Gratins   218

Harissa Aubergine and Chickpea Flatbreads   220

Carrot, Beetroot and Feta Gratin   222

Leek and Spinach Omelette   224

Mozzarella, Tomato and Basil Salad with Dough Balls   226

Spinach and Feta Tortilla Pies   180

Pea and Pesto Soup   182

Speedy Cauliflower Pilau   184

Falafel and Beetroot Pittas   186

Courgette and Cheddar Omelette   188

Spicy Sweetcorn Fondue   190

Creamy Pumpkin and Pine Nut Stuffed Pasta   192

Butternut Soup with Antipasti Peppers   194

Garlic and Herb Mushrooms with Potato Cakes   196

Easy Tomato and Basil Soup   198

Tomato and Mozzarella Sourdough Bruschetta   200

Rustic Chickpea and Tomato Dip   202

Aubergine, Brie and Tomato Melted Stacks   204

Simple Spinach and Feta Wraps   206

Spinach Tortelloni, Walnut and Blue Cheese Gratin   208

Pea, Feta and Mint Pilaf   210

Red Pepper and Goats' Cheese Bruschetta   212

Sweet Chilli Vegetable Stir-Fry   214

Speedy Chickpea Dahl   216

Antipasti Pepper, Caper and Spinach Pasta   218

Harissa Aubergine and Hummus Flatbreads   220

Carrot and Beetroot Couscous with Feta   222

Pan-Cooked Eggs with Spinach and Leeks   224

Herby Mozzarella and Tomato Naan Pizza   226

30 Spinach and Feta Filo Parcels

Serves 2

250 g (8 oz) spinach leaves, rinsed
125 g (4 oz) feta cheese, crumbled
large pinch of freshly grated nutmeg
2 tablespoons chopped parsley
4 sheets of filo pastry
4 tablespoons olive oil
salt and pepper
tomato and red onion salad, to serve

- Place the spinach in a large saucepan without any extra water, cover and cook for 2 minutes until wilted. Drain and squeeze out as much excess water as possible.

- Chop the spinach and mix with the feta, nutmeg and parsley in a bowl. Season with pepper (the feta is salty so check before adding salt).

- Place 2 sheets of filo pastry on top of one another and brush lightly with oil. Place half the filling at the end of the sheet, then fold over to make a triangle and continue folding until the filling is enclosed. Brush with oil. Repeat to make 1 more parcel.

- Place the parcels on a baking sheet and bake in a preheated oven, 200°C (400°F), Gas Mark 6, for 15 minutes until crisp and golden. Serve with tomato and red onion salad.

 Spinach and Feta Tortilla Pies

Divide 50 g (2 oz) baby spinach leaves, 125 g (4 oz) feta cheese, ½ finely sliced small red onion and 1 tablespoon chopped parsley between 2 soft flour tortillas, placing the mixture on one half only. Season with a little grated nutmeg and pepper (the feta is salty so there's no need to add salt). Fold the tortillas over the filling and press together firmly. Cook in a large frying pan for 5–8 minutes, turning once, until the tortillas are crisp and hot. Serve with tomato salad.

 Spinach and Feta Salad Tarts

Brush 4 sheets of filo pastry with olive oil, cut each sheet in half widthways and stack 4 pieces on top of each other at a slight angle to make a star. Repeat with the remaining 4 pieces. Place on a baking sheet and slightly scrunch the edges of the pastry. Brush with olive oil and sprinkle over 2 teaspoons sesame seeds. Bake in a preheated oven, 200°C (400°F), Gas Mark 6, for 10 minutes until golden. Meanwhile, mix together 50 g (2 oz) baby spinach leaves, 125 g (4 oz) crumbled feta cheese, 4 halved cherry tomatoes, 8 pitted black olives, ½ small thinly sliced red onion and 1 tablespoon chopped parsley in a bowl. Mix with 2 tablespoons French dressing, pile on to the cooked pastry cases and serve.

30 Pea, Leek and Potato Soup with Pesto and Cheesy Toasts

Serves 2

15 g (½ oz) butter
400 g (13 oz) potatoes, peeled and chopped
1 leek, trimmed, cleaned and sliced
600 ml (1 pint) hot vegetable stock
175 g (6 oz) frozen peas
1 tablespoon pesto
salt and pepper

For the toasts

2 slices of French bread
75 g (3 oz) Gruyère cheese, grated

- Heat the butter in a saucepan, add the potatoes and leek and cook for 5 minutes to soften. Add the stock and bring to the boil, then reduce the heat, cover and simmer for 20 minutes until the potatoes are tender, adding the peas for the final 5 minutes.

- Blend the soup with a stick blender or in a food processor until smooth. Heat through and season.

- Toast the bread slices on one side under a preheated grill, then turn the slices over, top with the cheese and grill until melted.

- Ladle the soup into 2 warm serving bowls, swirl through the pesto and serve with the toasts.

---

1 Pea and Pesto Soup
Heat 375 g (12 oz) frozen peas in 600 ml (1 pint) vegetable stock in a saucepan. Add 1 crushed garlic clove and simmer for 5 minutes. Blend with a stick blender, then season and stir in 2 tablespoons crème fraîche and 1 tablespoon pesto. Serve sprinkled with ready-made croûtons.

2 Chunky Pea, Leek and Pesto Soup
Heat 15 g (½ oz) butter in a saucepan, add 1 trimmed, cleaned and chopped leek and cook for 3 minutes until softened. Add 600 ml (1 pint) hot vegetable stock, 150 g (5 oz) frozen peas, 75 g (3 oz) shredded cabbage and 50 g (2 oz) small pasta shapes.

Bring to the boil, then reduce the heat, cover and simmer for 10 minutes until cooked through. Stir in 1 tablespoon pesto and serve with crusty bread.

30 Curried Cauliflower, Lentil and Rice Pot

Serves 4

2 tablespoons vegetable oil
1 large onion, sliced
2 teaspoons cumin seeds
2 tablespoons Jalfrezi curry paste
350 g (11½ oz) cauliflower, cut into florets
100 g (3½ oz) red lentils
150 g (5 oz) basmati rice
700 ml (1⅛ pints) hot vegetable stock
2 carrots, peeled and coarsely grated
50 g (2 oz) toasted cashew nuts
2 handfuls of coriander leaves, to garnish

- Heat the oil in a large saucepan, add the onion and cook for 5 minutes until softened. Add the cumin seeds and cook for 30 seconds, then add the curry paste and cook for 30 seconds.

- Add the cauliflower, red lentils, rice and stock. Bring to the boil, then reduce the heat, cover and simmer for 10–15 minutes until cooked through and the liquid has been absorbed.

- Stir in the grated carrots and heat for 2 minutes, adding a little hot water if the mixture is too dry. Sprinkle over the cashews and serve scattered with coriander leaves.

 Speedy Cauliflower Pilau

Heat 2 tablespoons vegetable oil in a large saucepan, add 300 g (10 oz) button mushrooms, 250 g (8 oz) small cauliflower florets and 2 teaspoons garlic purée and fry for 3 minutes until tender. Add 2 tablespoons medium curry paste, 300 ml (½ pint) hot vegetable stock and 100 g (3½ oz) frozen peas and simmer for 2 minutes, then stir in 2 x 250 g (8 oz) packs ready-cooked basmati rice and heat through. Stir in 150 g (5 oz) baby spinach leaves until wilted. Sprinkle over 50 g (2 oz) toasted flaked almonds. Serve with naan bread and natural yogurt.

 Easy Cauliflower and Lentil Pilau

Place 2 tablespoons medium curry paste, 2 tablespoons vegetable oil and 2 crushed garlic cloves in a large saucepan and fry for 1 minute. Add 350 g (11½ oz) cauliflower florets, 2 medium chopped courgettes, 250 g (8 oz) halved button mushrooms, 100 g (3½ oz) red lentils, 150 g (5 oz) basmati rice and 700 ml (1⅛ pints) hot vegetable stock and bring to the boil, then reduce the heat, cover and simmer for 10–15 minutes until the vegetables are tender and the stock has been absorbed. Stir in 2 coarsely grated carrots and 50 g (2 oz) toasted cashew nuts. Serve on warm chapattis with spoonfuls of natural yogurt.

MID-VEGE-LUD

30 Falafels with Beetroot Salad and Mint Yogurt

Serves 2

400 g (13 oz) can chickpeas, rinsed
and drained
½ small red onion, roughly chopped
1 garlic clove, chopped
½ red chilli, deseeded
1 teaspoon ground cumin
1 teaspoon ground coriander
handful of flat leaf parsley
2 tablespoons olive oil
salt and pepper

For the beetroot salad

1 carrot, coarsely grated
1 raw beetroot, coarsely grated
50 g (2 oz) baby spinach leaves
1 tablespoon lemon juice
2 tablespoons olive oil

For the mint yogurt

150 g (5 oz) Greek-style natural
yogurt
1 tablespoon chopped mint leaves
½ garlic clove, crushed

- To make the falafels, place the chickpeas, onion, garlic, chilli, cumin, coriander and parsley in a food processor. Season, then blend to make a coarse paste. Shape the mixture into 8 patties and set aside.

- To make the salad, place the carrot, beetroot and spinach in a bowl. Season, add the lemon juice and oil and stir well.

- To make the mint yogurt, mix all the ingredients together and season with a little salt.

- Heat the oil in a frying pan, add the falafels and fry for 4–5 minutes on each side until golden. Serve with the beetroot salad and mint yogurt.

 1 Falafel and Beetroot Pittas

Warm 4 shop-bought ready-made falafels in a preheated oven, 190°C (375°F), Gas Mark 5, for 5 minutes, adding 2 pitta breads for 2 minutes. Split open the pittas, then fill each with a small handful of watercress, some ready-cooked fresh beetroot slices, tomato slices and the falafels. Add a spoonful of ready-made tzatziki to each pitta and serve.

 2 Chickpea Burgers with Beetroot

Place a 400 g (13 oz) can chickpeas, rinsed and drained, 1 garlic clove, 1 teaspoon harissa paste or ½ teaspoon chilli powder and a small handful of flat leaf parsley in a food processor. Season, then blend to make a coarse paste. Shape the mixture into 4 burgers. Heat 2 tablespoons olive oil in a frying pan, add the burgers and fry for 4–5 minutes, turning once, until golden and heated through. Serve on toasted burger buns with spinach leaves, a spoonful of ready-made tzatziki and some chopped ready-cooked fresh beetroot. (If you don't want to cook all the burgers, they can be frozen.)

30 Cheesy Courgette Bakes

Serves 2

1 tablespoon olive oil
2 courgettes, chopped
1 garlic clove, crushed
4 spring onions, chopped
2 eggs
150 ml (¼ pint) single cream
1 teaspoon wholegrain mustard
125 g (4 oz) mature Cheddar
  cheese, grated
4 tablespoons fresh white
  breadcrumbs
1 tablespoon chopped parsley
salt and pepper

- Heat the oil in a frying pan, add the courgettes, garlic and spring onions and fry for 5 minutes until the courgettes are browned and just tender. Divide the mixture between 2 individual ovenproof dishes.

- Beat together the eggs, cream and mustard in a jug, then season. Stir in half the cheese and pour the mixture over the courgettes.

- Mix together the remaining cheese, the breadcrumbs and parsley in a bowl. Season and sprinkle over the egg mixture. Bake in a preheated oven, 200°C (400°F), Gas Mark 6, for 20 minutes until the tops are golden and the egg mixture has just set.

---

1 Courgette and Cheddar Omelette

Heat 1 tablespoon olive oil in a flameproof frying pan, add 2 chopped courgettes and 1 crushed garlic clove and fry for 3 minutes until tender. Beat together 6 eggs, 1 tablespoon water and 1 teaspoon wholegrain mustard in a jug, then season. Stir in 50 g (2 oz) grated mature Cheddar cheese, then pour over the courgettes. Cook for 2–3 minutes until the base is golden and set. Sprinkle over another 25 g (1 oz) grated Cheddar, then place the pan under a preheated medium grill for 2 minutes until the top is set and golden. Cut into wedges to serve.

2 Cheesy Courgette Carbonara

Cook 175 g (6 oz) spaghetti in a saucepan of lightly salted boiling water for 10 minutes, or until just tender. Meanwhile, heat 1 tablespoon olive oil in a frying pan, add 2 courgettes, cut into thin sticks, 1 crushed garlic clove and 4 spring onions, cut into thin sticks, and fry for 3–4 minutes until browned and tender. Beat together 2 eggs, 150 ml (¼ pint) single cream and 50 g (2 oz) grated Parmesan cheese in a jug, then season. Drain the spaghetti, add to the courgettes and pour over the beaten eggs. Mix well and gently heat through, taking care not to scramble the eggs. Serve with extra grated Parmesan and a grinding of black pepper.

Sweetcorn Fritters with Sweet Chilli Dip

Serves 4

250 g (8 oz) plain flour
2 eggs
125 ml (4 fl oz) milk
6 spring onions, chopped
2 x 325 g (11 oz) cans sweetcorn, drained well
2 tablespoons vegetable oil, plus extra if needed
salt and pepper
coriander leaves, to garnish

For the dip

250 g (8 oz) light soft cheese
2 tablespoons sweet chilli sauce

- Place the flour in a bowl and make a well in the centre. Break the eggs into the well and add the milk. Gradually whisk the flour into the eggs and milk to make a smooth, thick batter. Stir in the spring onions and sweetcorn and season.

- Heat the oil in a large frying pan, add spoonfuls of the batter, about 4 at a time, to the pan and cook for 2 minutes on each side until golden and firm to the touch. Remove from the pan and repeat with the remaining batter, adding extra oil if necessary.

- Meanwhile, make the dip. Stir the soft cheese in a bowl to soften, then lightly stir through the sweet chilli sauce to form a marbled effect. Serve the fritters with the dip, sprinkled with coriander leaves.

Spicy Sweetcorn Fondue

Bring 300 ml (½ pint) dry white wine to the boil in a large saucepan, then reduce the heat and add 250 g (8 oz) each of grated Gruyère cheese and Emmental cheese, a handful at a time, stirring until melted. Blend 2 teaspoons cornflour with 4 teaspoons cold water, then add to the pan and stir until thickened. Add 2 x 200 g (7 oz) cans sweetcorn, drained, 2 large pinches of cayenne pepper and salt and pepper. Serve hot with tortilla chips for dipping.

 Sweetcorn Rosti with Chilli Salsa

Par-boil 750 g (1½ lb) halved potatoes in a large saucepan of lightly salted boiling water for 10 minutes. Meanwhile, make the salsa. Chop 4 tomatoes and mix with 1 deseeded and finely chopped red chilli and 2 tablespoons chopped flat leaf parsley. Season, then add 2 tablespoons olive oil and 2 teaspoons balsamic vinegar. Set aside. Drain the potatoes and cool slightly. Coarsely grate the potatoes into a bowl and add 2 x 200 g (7 oz) cans sweetcorn, drained, 4 chopped spring onions, 250 g (8 oz) grated Emmental or Gruyère cheese and 2 beaten eggs. Season and mix lightly, then shape the mixture into 8 cakes. Heat 2 tablespoons olive oil in a large frying pan, add the cakes and cook for 5–8 minutes until crisp and golden, turning once. Serve with the chilli salsa.

MID-VEGE-HAS

30 Stuffed Pasta, Pine Nut and Butternut Gratin

Serves 2

250 g (8 oz) butternut squash, peeled, deseeded and sliced

1 tablespoon olive oil

2 garlic cloves, unpeeled

25 g (1 oz) pine nuts

250 g (8 oz) pack fresh four cheese tortelloni

150 ml (¼ pint) double cream

25 g (1 oz) grated Parmesan cheese

4 tablespoons fresh white breadcrumbs

4 sage leaves

salt and pepper

rocket and tomato salad, to serve (optional)

- Place the squash on a baking sheet, drizzle over the oil and season. Roast in a preheated oven, 200°C (400°F), Gas Mark 6, for 5 minutes. Add the garlic and pine nuts, return to the oven and cook for a further 15–20 minutes until the squash is tender, the garlic is soft and the pine nuts are toasted.

- Towards the end of the cooking time, cook the tortelloni in a saucepan of lightly salted boiling water for 3–4 minutes, or according to the packet instructions, until tender. Drain, tip into a flameproof dish with the roasted squash and pine nuts and gently toss together.

- Squeeze the soft garlic from its skin, mix with the cream and season. Spoon over the tortelloni and squash and sprinkle with the Parmesan, breadcrumbs and sage leaves. Place under a preheated medium grill for 2–3 minutes until golden and bubbling. Serve with a rocket and tomato salad, if liked.

 Creamy Pumpkin and Pine Nut Stuffed Pasta Cook a 250 g (8 oz) pack fresh pumpkin and pine nut pasta in a saucepan of lightly salted boiling water for 3–4 minutes until tender. Meanwhile, in a separate saucepan, heat 150 ml (¼ pint) double cream and 1 crushed garlic clove. Season and stir in 50 g (2 oz) baby spinach leaves. Drain the pasta and mix with the sauce. Serve sprinkled with grated Parmesan cheese.

 Creamy Squash, Pine Nuts and Stuffed Pasta Cook 250 g (8 oz) peeled, deseeded and chopped butternut squash in a saucepan of lightly salted boiling water for 10 minutes until tender. Heat 1 tablespoon olive oil in a frying pan. Drain the squash, add to the frying pan and cook for 5 minutes, stirring occasionally until golden. Add 1 crushed garlic clove, 25 g (1 oz) pine nuts and 4 sage leaves and cook for 2 minutes. Meanwhile, in a separate saucepan, cook a 250 g (8 oz) pack fresh spinach and ricotta tortelloni in lightly salted boiling water for 3–4 minutes until tender, then drain and add to the squash with 150 ml (¼ pint) double cream. Heat through for 2 minutes until bubbling, season and serve sprinkled with grated Parmesan cheese.

Spiced Butternut Squash Soup

Serves 4

500 g (1 lb) butternut squash, peeled and chopped

250 g (8 oz) parsnips, peeled and chopped

250 g (8 oz) celeriac, peeled and chopped

2 teaspoons ground cumin

2 teaspoons ginger purée from a jar or tube

1.2 litres (2 pints) hot vegetable stock

4 tablespoons crème fraîche

salt and pepper

flat leaf parsley, to garnish

• Place the vegetables, spices and stock in a large saucepan. Bring to the boil, then reduce the heat, cover and simmer for 15 minutes until tender. Blend with a stick blender until almost smooth and season.

• Ladle the soup into 4 warm serving bowls and add a spoonful of crème fraîche to each one. Serve scattered with flat leaf parsley.

Butternut Soup with Antipasti Peppers Heat 2 tablespoons olive oil in a large saucepan, add 1 teaspoon cumin seeds and fry until they start 'popping'. Add 2 x 600 g (1 lb 5 oz) pots chilled butternut squash soup and 150 g (5 oz) chopped antipasti peppers from a jar. Heat through and serve topped with spoonfuls of crème fraîche and a sprinkle of smoked paprika. Serve with cheese straws.

Roasted Butternut and Red Pepper Soup Place 500 g (1 lb) peeled, deseeded and chopped butternut squash, 2 cored, deseeded and chopped red peppers and 2 chopped onions in a large roasting tin. Drizzle with 2 tablespoons olive oil, sprinkle with 2 teaspoons cumin seeds and season. Roast in a preheated oven, 220°C (425°F), Gas Mark 7, for 20 minutes until tender, adding 2 chopped garlic cloves for the final 5 minutes. Tip the vegetables into a large saucepan and add 1.2 litres (2 pints) hot vegetable stock, bring to the boil, then reduce the heat and simmer for 5 minutes. Blend with a stick blender until almost smooth. Serve topped with spoonfuls of crème fraîche and scattered with flat leaf parsley.

30 Garlic and Herb Mushroom Tart

Serves 2

25 g (1 oz) butter
1 garlic clove, crushed
150 g (5 oz) button mushrooms, halved
2 tablespoons chopped parsley
1 teaspoon thyme leaves
½ x 375 g (12 oz) sheet of ready-rolled shortcrust pastry
125 g (4 oz) ricotta cheese
1 tablespoon sun-dried tomato paste
beaten egg, to glaze
50 g (2 oz) grated Manchego cheese
salt and pepper

- Heat the butter in a frying pan, add the garlic and mushrooms and cook for 3–5 minutes, stirring, until browned. Add the parsley and thyme and season. Remove from the heat.

- Place the pastry on a baking sheet. Mix together the ricotta and tomato paste and spread over the pastry, leaving a 2.5 cm (1 inch) border around the edge. Top with the mushroom mixture.

- Brush the border with a little beaten egg. Fold the border up over the edge of the filling, loosely scrunching or folding it as you go round. Brush the pastry with beaten egg and sprinkle the Manchego over the filling and pastry.

- Bake in a preheated oven, 200°C (400°F), Gas Mark 6, for 15 minutes until the pastry is golden.

 Garlic and Herb Mushrooms with Potato Cakes Heat 25 g (1 oz) garlic and herb butter in a frying pan, add 175 g (6 oz) button mushrooms and cook for 3 minutes. Add 25 g (1 oz) chopped sun-dried tomatoes and 4 tablespoons crème fraîche and season. Heat through, adding a little milk if the sauce is too thick. Heat 2 shop-bought potato cakes in a toaster or under a preheated grill, spoon the mushroom mixture over the top and serve sprinkled with sliced Manchego cheese and chopped parsley.

 Garlic, Herb and Brie Stuffed Mushrooms Heat 50 g (2 oz) butter in a frying pan, add the chopped stalks from 4 large portobello mushrooms and 1 crushed garlic clove and cook for 2 minutes. Stir in 1 tablespoon chopped parsley and 1 teaspoon chopped thyme leaves and season. Place the mushrooms on a baking tray, stalk side up. Spoon the garlic and herb mixture on to the mushrooms. Top each with 1 tablespoon tomato and basil pasta sauce, 2 halved cherry tomatoes and 25 g (1 oz) chopped brie. Bake in a preheated oven, 200°C (400°F), Gas Mark 6, for 15 minutes until the mushrooms are tender. Sprinkle with a little extra chopped parsley and serve with crusty bread to mop up the juices.

Mediterranean Tomato Soup

Serves 2

375 g (12 oz) ripe tomatoes, roughly chopped

5 tablespoons olive oil

1 garlic clove, crushed

300 ml (½ pint) hot vegetable stock

1 tablespoon tomato purée

½ teaspoon caster sugar

1 teaspoon oregano leaves, plus extra leaves to garnish

1 tablespoon shredded basil leaves

1 ciabatta roll, torn into pieces

2 tablespoons grated Parmesan cheese

salt and pepper

- Place the tomatoes in a saucepan with 2 tablespoons of the oil and the garlic. Cook for 3 minutes until softened, then add the stock, tomato purée, sugar, oregano and shredded basil. Bring to the boil, then reduce the heat, cover and simmer for 10 minutes.

- Meanwhile, spread the ciabatta pieces over a baking sheet and drizzle over 2 tablespoons of the oil. Toast under a preheated medium grill for a few minutes, turning occasionally, until crisp and golden.

- Blend the soup with a stick blender until smooth. Stir in half the Parmesan and season.

- Ladle the soup into 2 warm serving bowls, drizzle with the remaining oil and top with some of the ciabatta croûtons. Scatter with the remaining Parmesan and a few oregano leaves. Serve with the remaining croûtons.

 Easy Tomato and Basil Soup

Place 375 g (12 oz) ripe tomatoes, 1 peeled garlic clove, 150 ml (¼ pint) passata, 2 slices of ciabatta bread, crusts removed, 2 tablespoons pesto, 1 tablespoon olive oil, 1 teaspoon white wine vinegar and a pinch of caster sugar in a food processor. Blend until smooth, then pour into a saucepan and heat through for 3–4 minutes until piping hot. Season, then serve with ciabatta toast.

 Tomato and Bean Soup

Heat 1 tablespoon olive oil in a saucepan, add 1 small chopped onion, 1 peeled and chopped carrot and ½ chopped courgette and cook for 5 minutes. Add 300 ml (½ pint) passata and 300 ml (½ pint) hot vegetable stock and bring to the boil, then reduce the heat and simmer for 20 minutes until the vegetables are tender, adding 75 g (3 oz) shredded curly kale for the final 5 minutes. Stir in 175 g (6 oz) canned cannellini beans and 1 tablespoon shredded basil leaves and heat through. Season and serve with crusty bread.

Tomato and Mozzarella Sourdough Bruschetta

Serves 2

2 thick slices of sourdough bread
4 tablespoons olive oil
½ teaspoon salt flakes
1 small red onion, cut into slim wedges
½ teaspoon cumin seeds
175 g (6 oz) baby plum tomatoes, halved
125 g (4 oz) pot mozzarella pearls, drained
1 tablespoon chopped coriander leaves, to garnish

- Lightly brush each of the sourdough slices with oil, sprinkle with the salt flakes and toast under a preheated hot grill for 30 seconds–1 minute on each side until golden.

- Meanwhile, heat the remaining oil in a frying pan, add the onion and cumin seeds and cook over a medium heat for 5 minutes, stirring occasionally, until golden and softened.

- Add the tomatoes and cook for a further 1 minute, taking care not to let them lose their shape. Add the mozzarella and remove the pan from the heat, shaking it a little to warm the cheese very slightly.

- Divide the mixture between the toasts and serve scattered with the coriander.

---

2 Warm Tomato and Mozzarella Salad with Sourdough Croûtons

Place 175 g (6 oz) halved cherry tomatoes and 150 g (5 oz) thinly sliced mozzarella cheese in a bowl. Heat 2 tablespoons olive oil in a frying pan, add 1 thinly sliced red onion and 1 teaspoon cumin seeds and cook over a medium heat for 5 minutes until golden and softened. Add the onion mixture to the mozzarella and tomatoes, tossing until all the ingredients are slightly warmed. Arrange on 2 serving plates. Heat 2 tablespoons olive oil in a small frying pan, add 1 cubed slice of sourdough bread and fry over a high heat for 1 minute, turning frequently, until golden. Scatter over the salad to serve.

3 Tomato and Mozzarella Sourdough Bake

Drizzle 4 thin slices of sourdough bread with 4 tablespoons olive oil. Heat 1 tablespoon olive oil in a frying pan, add 1 small thinly sliced onion and 1 teaspoon cumin seeds and cook over a medium heat for 3 minutes, stirring occasionally, until golden and softened. In a lightly greased small, shallow ovenproof dish, layer the bread slices with 4 thinly sliced tomatoes, the warm onions and 150 g (5 oz) thinly sliced mozzarella cheese, finishing with a layer of cheese. Bake in a preheated oven, 200°C (400°F), Gas Mark 6, for 15 minutes until golden and hot.

# Chickpea, Artichoke and Tomato Pan-Fry

Serves 4

2 x 400 g (13 oz) can chickpeas, rinsed and drained

2 x 400 g (13 oz) can artichokes, drained and halved

5 tablespoons olive oil

1 bunch of spring onions, roughly chopped

2 teaspoons ground cumin

3 fresh tomatoes, cut into slim wedges

12 sun-blush tomatoes in oil, drained, plus 2 tablespoons of the oil

3 tablespoons mixed fresh herbs

pepper

To serve

3 tablespoons grated Parmesan cheese

warm crusty bread

- Place the chickpeas in a bowl and lightly crush with a potato masher. Season well with pepper.

- Place the artichokes on a foil-lined grill rack and drizzle with 2 tablespoons of the olive oil. Cook under a preheated hot grill for 5 minutes until lightly charred in places. Set aside.

- Heat the remaining oil in a large frying pan, add the spring onions, cumin, fresh tomatoes and chickpeas and cook over a high heat for 5 minutes, then add the sun-blush tomatoes and oil, herbs and artichokes and toss well.

- Serve in 4 warm serving bowls with the Parmesan sprinkled over and warm crusty bread to mop up the juices.

Rustic Chickpea and Tomato Dip

Place 2 x 400 g (13 oz) cans chickpeas, rinsed and drained, 125 ml (4 fl oz) olive oil, 8 roughly chopped spring onions, 12 sun-blush tomatoes in oil, drained, plus 2 tablespoons of the oil, 4 tablespoons snipped chives and 4 tablespoons chopped basil leaves in a food processor. Season well and whizz until almost smooth but still textured. Serve with crudités and breadsticks.

Warm Chickpea, Artichoke and Tomato Stew

Heat 2 tablespoons olive oil in a large saucepan, add 1 large roughly chopped onion, 2 teaspoons ground cumin, 2 teaspoons ground coriander and 1 teaspoon ground paprika and cook for 3 minutes, then add 2 x 400 g (13 oz) cans chickpeas, rinsed and drained, 2 x 400 g (13 oz) cans artichokes, drained, 3 fresh tomatoes, cut into slim wedges, 600 ml (1 pint) hot vegetable stock and 12 drained and roughly chopped sun-blush tomatoes in oil. Bring to the boil, then reduce the heat, cover and simmer for 20 minutes, stirring occasionally. Season well and serve.

30 Asparagus, Aubergine, Brie and Tomato Quiche

Serves 2

½ x 350 g (11½ oz) sheet of ready-rolled shortcrust pastry

4 tablespoons olive oil

½ small aubergine, cubed

125 g (4 oz) asparagus spears, trimmed and cut into 5 cm (2 inch) lengths

125 g (4 oz) brie, cut into chunks

6 sun-blush tomatoes in oil, drained

100 ml (3½ fl oz) milk

3 eggs

2 tablespoons chopped thyme leaves

salt and pepper

simple dressed salad, to serve

- Use the pastry to line a 30 x 15 cm (12 x 6 inch) fluted flan tin and trim the edges. Chill in the refrigerator.

- Heat the oil in a large frying pan, add the aubergine and cook over a high heat for 5 minutes until golden and soft, then add the asparagus and cook for a further 2 minutes until a little golden.

- Arrange the brie, tomatoes, aubergine and asparagus in the pastry-lined tin. Mix together the milk, eggs and thyme in a jug, season well and pour into the pastry case.

- Place in the top of a preheated oven, 220°C (425°F), Gas Mark 7, for 20 minutes until golden and set. Serve warm with a simple dressed salad.

---

1 Aubergine, Brie and Tomato Melted Stacks Cut 1 small aubergine into 5 mm (¼ inch) slices. Heat 6 tablespoons olive oil in a very large frying pan, add all the aubergine slices and cook for 2 minutes on each side until golden and soft. On a foil-lined grill rack, layer the slices with 125 g (4 oz) sliced brie and 8 drained sun-blush tomatoes in oil to form 2 stacks, finishing with a slice of brie. Cook under a preheated hot grill for about 1 minute until the cheese has melted and the stacks are warm. Serve with a simple salad.

2 Asparagus, Aubergine, Brie and Tomato Tortilla Heat 4 tablespoons olive oil in a large, flameproof frying pan, add ½ small cubed aubergine and cook over a high heat for 5 minutes until golden and soft. Add 125 g (4 oz) asparagus spears, trimmed and cut into 5 cm (2 inch) lengths, and cook for a further 3 minutes, then add 6 drained and roughly chopped sun-blush tomatoes in oil and stir well. Remove from the heat. In a jug, beat together 5 eggs and 5 tablespoons milk and season well. Add 2 tablespoons chopped thyme leaves and beat again. Pour the egg mixture into the pan and mix well to evenly distribute the vegetables, then scatter over 75 g (3 oz) cubed brie. Return to the heat and cook gently for 5 minutes until the base is set, then place the pan under a preheated hot grill and cook for 4–5 minutes until golden and set. Serve in wedges with a simple dressed salad.

Warm Spinach and Feta Tortilla Slices

Serves 2

3 tablespoons olive oil

1 small red onion, thinly sliced

1 garlic clove, roughly chopped

250 g (8 oz) spinach leaves

200 g (7 oz) feta cheese, crumbled

4 tablespoons mascarpone cheese

1 tablespoon sunflower oil

2 large soft flour tortillas

2 tablespoons grated Parmesan cheese

salt and pepper

- Heat the olive oil in a large, flameproof frying pan, add the onion and garlic and cook over a medium-high heat for 3–4 minutes until golden and softened. Add the spinach and stir well for 1–2 minutes until wilted.

- Drain off any excess juices from the pan and transfer the spinach mixture to a bowl. Stir in the feta and mascarpone and season well.

- Rinse out the pan and add the sunflower oil. Place a tortilla in the pan and evenly spoon over the spinach mixture, then place the second tortilla on top. Press down well, then scatter over the Parmesan.

- Place the pan over the heat and cook for 2–3 minutes, then place under a preheated hot grill and cook for 2 minutes until golden and the cheese has melted. Serve cut into wedges.

Simple Spinach and Feta Wraps

Heat 3 tablespoons olive oil in a small frying pan, add 1 small thinly sliced red onion and cook over a medium heat for 3–4 minutes until softened. Transfer to a bowl and stir in 75 g (3 oz) shredded spinach leaves and 200 g (7 oz) crumbled feta cheese. Place 2 soft flour tortillas on a board and spread each with 1 tablespoon chutney of your choice, then add the spinach and feta mixture. Roll up the tortillas tightly and cut in half to serve.

Spinach and Feta Burritos

Heat 2 tablespoons olive oil in a frying pan, add 1 thinly sliced red onion and 1 roughly chopped garlic clove and cook over a medium heat for 3 minutes until golden and softened. Add 250 g (8 oz) spinach leaves and cook, stirring and tossing, for 2–3 minutes until wilted. Remove from the heat and add 3 tablespoons mascarpone cheese and 200 g (7 oz) crumbled feta cheese and mix well. Divide the filling evenly between 2 soft flour tortillas, make 1 or 2 folds to enclose the filling and place in a shallow ovenproof dish. Scatter with 75 g (3 oz) grated mature Cheddar cheese and bake in a preheated oven, 200°C (400°F), Gas Mark 6, for 15 minutes until melted and pale golden. Serve with a simple salad.

Spinach Tortelloni, Walnut and Blue Cheese Gratin

Serves 2

300 g (10 oz) pack fresh spinach and ricotta tortelloni

375 g (12 oz) pot fresh cheese sauce

1 teaspoon ground nutmeg

50 g (2 oz) fresh wholemeal breadcrumbs

50 g (2 oz) walnuts, roughly chopped

75 g (3 oz) blue cheese, very well crumbled

simple salad, to serve

- Cook the tortelloni in a large saucepan of lightly salted boiling water for 3 minutes, or according to the packet instructions. Drain well, then return to the pan. Add the cheese sauce and ground nutmeg and heat through.

- Transfer to a shallow gratin dish and level the top. Mix the breadcrumbs with the walnuts and blue cheese, then scatter over the pasta.

- Cook under a preheated hot grill for 2–3 minutes until the top is golden and melted. Serve with a simple salad.

 Blue Cheese, Spinach and Walnut Tart Place ½ x 350 g (11½ oz) sheet of ready-rolled shortcrust pastry on a baking sheet, lift up the 4 corners and pinch together to form a base, then lightly prick with a fork. Place in a preheated oven, 200°C (400°F), Gas Mark 6, for 12–15 minutes until golden. Meanwhile, heat 1 tablespoon olive oil in a frying pan, add 1 small thinly sliced onion and cook for 3–4 minutes until softened, then add 175 g (6 oz) spinach leaves and ½ teaspoon ground nutmeg. Fill the case with the spinach mixture and 75 g (3 oz) crumbled blue cheese, then top with 1 tablespoon finely chopped walnuts. Return to the oven for 2–3 minutes. Serve in slices.

 Blue Cheese, Spinach and Walnut Gnocchi Bake Heat 25 g (1 oz) butter in a saucepan, add 50 g (2 oz) roughly chopped walnuts and cook over a medium heat for 2 minutes until turning golden, then add 25 g (1 oz) plain flour and cook for 30 seconds, stirring. Remove from the heat and gradually add 300 ml (½ pint) milk. Return to the heat, add 1 teaspoon ground nutmeg and bring to the boil, stirring continuously until boiled and thickened. Remove from the heat, add 125 g (4 oz) baby spinach leaves and 100 g (3½ oz) crumbled blue cheese and stir well until the spinach is wilted and the cheese is melted. Meanwhile, cook 300 g (10 oz) pack fresh gnocchi in a saucepan of lightly salted boiling water for 3 minutes, or according to the packet instructions. Drain well, then add to the pan and stir to coat. Transfer to a shallow ovenproof dish and scatter with 3 tablespoons grated Parmesan cheese. Place at the top of a preheated oven, 220°C (425°F), Gas Mark 7, for 15 minutes until bubbling. Serve with a simple salad and crusty bread, if liked.

 # Pea, Parmesan and Mint Risotto

Serves 2

2 tablespoons olive oil

1 onion, thinly sliced

175 g (6 oz) risotto rice

600 ml (1 pint) hot vegetable stock

6 tablespoons grated Parmesan cheese

125 g (4 oz) frozen peas

3 tablespoons chopped mint leaves

½ Little Gem lettuce, thinly shredded

salt and pepper

warm crusty bread, to serve

- Heat the oil in a frying pan, add the onion and cook over a medium heat for 3 minutes until softened. Add the rice and cook, stirring, for 2 minutes.

- Pour in all the stock and bring to the boil, then reduce the heat, cover and simmer very gently for 15 minutes until the rice is tender, stirring occasionally and adding a little more water if necessary.

- Add the Parmesan, peas and mint and cook for a further 3 minutes until the peas have defrosted. Stir in the shredded lettuce and stir well, then season well. Serve with warm crusty bread.

Pea, Feta and Mint Pilaf

Heat a 250 g (8 oz) pack ready-cooked long-grain rice according to the packet instructions. Meanwhile, heat 2 tablespoons olive oil in a frying pan, add 1 small thinly sliced onion and cook for 3–4 minutes until softened. Add 125 g (4 oz) frozen peas and 4 tablespoons water and cook for 2 minutes until hot, then add the rice and crumble in 200 g (7 oz) feta cheese and 2 tablespoons chopped mint leaves. Toss well and serve.

Cheesy Pea and Mint Rice Balls

Place 125 g (4 oz) soft cheese and a 250 g (8 oz) pack ready-cooked long-grain rice in a bowl and mix well. Add 1 egg yolk, 75 g (3 oz) defrosted peas, 1 tablespoon chopped mint leaves and season well. Mix well until firm, then shape into 8 balls. Roll in 50 g (2 oz) fresh white breadcrumbs to lightly coat. Heat 2 tablespoons olive oil in a frying pan, add the balls and cook for 3–4 minutes, turning frequently, until golden. Serve hot with a simple salad.

30 Goats' Cheese and Butternut Squash Stuffed Peppers

Serves 2

2 tablespoons olive oil

2 red peppers, halved, cored and deseeded

175 g (6 oz) butternut squash, peeled, deseeded and cut into small chunks

1 small red onion, roughly chopped

2 tablespoons black olive tapenade

75 g (3 oz) soft goats' cheese, crumbled

2 tablespoons fresh breadcrumbs

1 tablespoon grated Parmesan cheese

To serve

simple salad

crusty bread (optional)

- Heat 1 tablespoon of the oil in a large frying pan, add the peppers, cut side down, and cook for 2 minutes, then turn the peppers over and cook for a further 2 minutes. Remove from the pan.

- Meanwhile, heat the remaining oil in a separate frying pan, add the squash and onion and cook for 5 minutes until slightly softened. Remove from the pan and toss with the tapenade in a bowl, then add the goats' cheese and gently toss together.

- Spoon the mixture into the pepper halves, then place the peppers in a roasting tin and scatter with the breadcrumbs and Parmesan.

- Place in a preheated oven, 200°C (400°F), Gas Mark 6, for 15 minutes until the tops are golden and cooked through. Serve hot with a simple salad and crusty bread, if liked.

 Red Pepper and Goats' Cheese Bruschetta Heat 3 tablespoons olive oil in a frying pan, add 1 small thinly sliced red onion and 1 cored, deseeded and roughly chopped red pepper and cook for 5 minutes. Meanwhile, lightly toast 2 slices of soda bread on both sides until crisp, then spread each with 1 tablespoon black olive tapenade. Top with the red pepper mixture, arrange 125 g (4 oz) soft rind goats' cheese on top and serve.

 Red Pepper, Butternut and Goats' Cheese Soup Heat 2 tablespoons olive oil in a frying pan, add 1 cored, deseeded and roughly chopped red pepper and 300 g (10 oz) peeled and deseeded butternut squash, cut into pieces, and cook for 10 minutes until softened and golden in places. Place in a food processor with 300 ml (½ pint) hot chicken stock and 125 g (4 oz) soft goats' cheese and whizz until smooth. Season well and serve.

MID-VEGE-NAO

Tempura Mixed Vegetables with Chilli Sauce

Serves 4

vegetable oil, for deep-frying
1 large red pepper, cored,
    deseeded and cut into chunks
150 g (5 oz) baby corn
150 g (5 oz) broccoli florets
100 g (3½ oz) asparagus spears,
    trimmed
6 large spring onions, cut into
    5 cm (2 inch) lengths
chilli dipping sauce, to serve

For the batter

25 g (1 oz) plain flour
50 g (2 oz) cornflour
2 eggs, beaten
75 ml (3 fl oz) beer
salt

- Sift the flour and cornflour into a bowl and season with a little salt. Make a well in the centre, add the eggs and whisk a little, then gradually add the beer, pouring it in slowly and whisking continuously to make a smooth batter.

- Half fill a deep saucepan with vegetable oil and heat to 190°C (375°F), or until a cube of bread browns in 30 seconds. Working quickly, dip the vegetable pieces, one by one, into the batter. Deep-fry in batches in the hot oil for 1–2 minutes until lightly golden. Remove with a slotted spoon, drain on kitchen paper and keep warm. Serve with chilli dipping sauce.

 **Sweet Chilli Vegetable Stir-Fry**

Heat 3 tablespoons sesame oil in a large wok or frying pan, add 1 cored, deseeded and roughly chopped red pepper, 250 g (8 oz) baby corn, halved lengthways, and 100 g (3½ oz) very small broccoli florets and stir-fry over a high heat for 3 minutes. Add 12 roughly chopped spring onions and 12 asparagus spears, trimmed and cut into 5 cm (2 inch) lengths, and stir-fry for a further 3 minutes until tender and lightly charred in places.

Add 6 tablespoons sweet chilli sauce and 3 tablespoons soy sauce and cook for 1 minute, stirring continuously until piping hot. Serve with ready-cooked rice, if liked.

Sweet Chilli and Tempura Vegetable Noodles Cook the Tempura Mixed Vegetables as above. Meanwhile, cook 200 g (7 oz) soba noodles and 150 g (5 oz) trimmed fine green beans in a saucepan of lightly salted boiling water for 10 minutes until tender. Drain well. In a large wok, toss the tempura with the noodles and beans. Mix together 125 ml (4 fl oz) sweet chilli sauce, 3 tablespoons soy sauce and 3 tablespoons sesame oil in a small bowl, then toss into the noodles. Serve hot.

Red Lentil Dahl with Warm Naan

Serves 4

2 tablespoons groundnut oil

2 large onions, thinly sliced

1 red pepper, cored, deseeded and sliced

4 tomatoes, roughly chopped

2 garlic cloves, roughly chopped

4 teaspoons curry powder

2 teaspoons turmeric

300 g (10 oz) red lentils

900 ml (1½ pints) hot vegetable stock

4 mini naan breads

salt and pepper

roughly chopped coriander leaves, to garnish

natural yogurt, to serve

- Heat the oil in a large frying pan, add the onions and red pepper and cook over a medium heat for 3 minutes until starting to soften. Add the tomatoes and garlic and cook for a further 2 minutes, then add the curry powder, turmeric and lentils and stir well.

- Pour in the stock and bring to the boil. Reduce the heat, cover and simmer gently for 15 minutes until the lentils are completely cooked through and soft, adding a little more water if necessary. Season well.

- Meanwhile, heat the naans in a preheated oven, 180°C (350°F), Gas Mark 4, for 5–8 minutes, or until warm.

- Spoon the dahl on to the warm naans, scatter with chopped coriander and serve with spoonfuls of yogurt.

 Speedy Chickpea Dahl

Heat 2 tablespoons groundnut oil in a large saucepan, add 1 chopped onion and cook over a medium heat for 3 minutes, then add 2 teaspoons curry powder and 1 teaspoon turmeric. Stir in 2 x 400 g (13 oz) cans chickpeas, rinsed and drained. Remove from the heat and mash the chickpeas with a potato masher, breaking them up well. Pour in 600 ml (1 pint) hot vegetable stock and bring to the boil, then reduce the heat, cover and simmer for 3 minutes. Serve with naan breads and chopped coriander leaves.

Yellow Lentil Dahl

Heat 2 tablespoons groundnut oil in a large frying pan, add 2 large roughly chopped onions and cook over a medium heat for 3 minutes until slightly softened. Add 2 teaspoons cumin seeds, 4 teaspoons curry powder, 2 teaspoons turmeric and 4 roughly chopped tomatoes and cook for 1 minute, then add 300 g (10 oz) yellow lentils. Stir in 900 ml (1½ pints) hot vegetable stock and bring to the boil, then reduce the heat, cover and simmer for 25 minutes, adding 2 handfuls of fresh spinach leaves for the final 3 minutes. Add a little water if it is too dry. Serve with warm naan breads and spoonfuls of natural yogurt.

Pepper, Caper and Spinach Pappardelle Gratins

Serves 4

350 g (11½ oz) pappardelle

1 red pepper, cored, deseeded and cut into chunks

1 yellow pepper, cored, deseeded and cut into chunks

2 tablespoons olive oil

100 g (3½ oz) black olives, pitted and roughly chopped

4 tablespoons drained capers

250 g (8 oz) baby spinach leaves

300 g (10 oz) mozzarella cheese, cubed

4 tablespoons grated Parmesan cheese

- Cook the pappardelle in a large saucepan of lightly salted boiling water for 8–10 minutes, or until just tender.

- Meanwhile, place the peppers in a roasting tin and toss with the oil. Cook under a preheated hot grill for 5 minutes, turning until lightly charred and soft.

- Drain the pasta and return to the pan with the olives, capers, spinach and mozzarella and toss over a low heat for 1 minute until the spinach wilts and the mozzarella starts to melt. Add the grilled peppers with the oil and toss.

- Pile into 4 flameproof serving bowls and sprinkle each with Parmesan, then place under a preheated hot grill for 1 minute until the tops are golden. Serve hot.

Antipasti Pepper, Caper and Spinach

Pasta Cook 600 g (1 lb 5 oz) fresh pasta in a large saucepan of lightly salted boiling water for 3 minutes, or according to the packet instructions. Drain well, then add 2 x 280 g (9 oz) jars antipasti peppers, drained, 75 g (3 oz) pitted and chopped black olives and 4 tablespoons drained capers. Toss well and heat for 2 minutes until piping hot. Season well and serve with 2 handfuls of baby spinach leaves stirred through.

Pepper, Caper and Spinach

Penne Bake Core, deseed and cut 2 red peppers and 2 yellow peppers into chunks, then toss with 2 tablespoons olive oil. Cook under a preheated hot grill for 5 minutes until lightly charred and softened. Meanwhile, cook 350 g (11½ oz) penne in a large saucepan of lightly salted boiling water for 8–10 minutes, or until just tender. Drain, then return to the pan and toss with the grilled peppers and 75 g (3 oz) pitted and roughly chopped black olives, 250 g (8 oz) baby spinach leaves and 4 tablespoons drained capers. Transfer to a large, shallow gratin dish and top with 300 g (10 oz) very thinly sliced mozzarella cheese. Scatter with 8 tablespoons fresh breadcrumbs and place at the top of a preheated oven, 220°C (425°F), Gas Mark 7, for 15 minutes until golden and bubbling. Serve with a simple green salad.

 # Harissa Aubergine and Hummus Flatbreads

Serves 2

1 small aubergine, cut into small cubes

1 tablespoon harissa paste

4 tablespoons olive oil

2 soft flatbreads or chapattis

6 tablespoons shop-bought hummus

40 g (1½ oz) rocket leaves

4 tablespoons chopped coriander leaves

- Place the aubergine and harissa in a bowl and toss to lightly coat. Heat the oil in a large frying pan, add the aubergine and cook over a medium-high heat for 5–7 minutes until softened and cooked through.

- Meanwhile, warm the flatbreads in a microwave for 30 seconds. Place on 2 warm serving plates and spread with the hummus. Top with the aubergine, then scatter with the rocket and coriander and serve.

 Harissa Aubergine and Chickpea Flatbreads Heat 4 tablespoons olive oil in a large frying pan, add 1 small sliced aubergine and 1 small thinly sliced red onion and cook over a high heat for 5 minutes until softened. Add 1 tablespoon harissa paste, 1 teaspoon ground coriander and a 400 g (13 oz) can chickpeas, rinsed and drained, and cook over a medium heat for a further 2 minutes until hot. Stir in 200 g (7 oz) canned chopped tomatoes, cover and cook for 5 minutes until the sauce is thick and pulpy. Season well, then scatter with 3 tablespoons chopped coriander leaves. Spoon on to 2 warm flatbreads and roll up to serve, if liked.

Harissa Aubergine and Chickpea Dip with Flatbread Crisps Cut 3 flatbreads into triangles, lightly brush each with a little olive oil and sprinkle each with a few salt flakes. Place on a baking sheet and bake in a preheated oven, 200°C (400°F), Gas Mark 6, for 5–6 minutes until golden. Leave to cool. Meanwhile, heat 4 tablespoons olive oil in a large frying pan, add 1 small cubed aubergine and 1 roughly chopped red onion and cook over a medium-high heat for 5 minutes. Add 1 tablespoon harissa paste and cook for a further 1 minute. Transfer the mixture to a food processor, add the finely grated rind and juice of 1 lemon and 1 teaspoon ground coriander and whizz until smooth. Return to the pan, add a 400 g (13 oz) can chickpeas, rinsed and drained, and stir for 2 minutes until piping hot. Serve the warm dip sprinkled with chopped coriander leaves, with the crisps.

MID-VEGE-BOO

30 Roasted Carrot and Beetroot Pearl Barley with Feta

Serves 4

2 red onions, cut into slim wedges

16 bunched carrots, scrubbed and cut into chunks

1 large raw beetroot, about 300 g (10 oz), peeled and cut into slim wedges

olive oil

1½ teaspoons cumin seeds

1½ teaspoons ground coriander

1½ chicken stock cubes

275 g (9 oz) pearl barley

300 g (10 oz) feta cheese, crumbled

6 tablespoons coriander leaves

- Place all the prepared vegetables in a large roasting tin, drizzle with the oil and toss to coat. Add the cumin seeds and ground coriander and toss again. Place at the top of a preheated oven, 220°C (425°F), Gas Mark 7, for 20–25 minutes until the vegetables are tender and lightly charred in places.

- Meanwhile, bring a large saucepan of lightly salted water to the boil, add the stock cubes and pearl barley and cook for 20 minutes until the grain is tender. Drain, then toss with the vegetables. Add the crumbled feta and coriander leaves, toss well and serve.

 1 **Carrot and Beetroot Couscous with Feta** Place 175 g (6 oz) couscous in a heatproof bowl and just cover with boiling water. Cover with clingfilm and leave to stand for 5 minutes. Meanwhile, heat 3 tablespoons olive oil in a large frying pan, add 375 g (12 oz) peeled and thinly sliced carrots and cook for 5 minutes, stirring frequently, until softened. Add 1½ teaspoons cumin seeds and ¾ teaspoon ground coriander and cook for a further 1 minute, then add the couscous, 275 g (9 oz) shop-bought ready-cooked fresh beetroot, roughly chopped, and a handful of rocket leaves. Toss together, then serve topped with 275 g (9 oz) crumbled feta cheese.

 2 **Carrot, Beetroot and Feta Gratin** Heat 3 tablespoons olive oil in a large frying pan, add 1 large thinly sliced red onion, 550 g (1 lb 2 oz) peeled and sliced carrots and 300 g (10 oz) raw beetroot, peeled and cut into slim wedges, and cook for 8–10 minutes until tender and cooked through. Add 1½ teaspoons cumin seeds and ¾ teaspoon ground coriander, then toss and cook for a further 2 minutes. Divide between 4 small gratin dishes, then scatter 300 g (10 oz) crumbled feta cheese over the tops. Cook under a preheated hot grill for 2–3 minutes until the feta has turned golden in places. Serve with warm crusty bread.

Pan-Cooked Eggs with Spinach and Leeks

Serves 2

25 g (1 oz) butter
1 leek, trimmed, cleaned and
   thinly sliced
¼ teaspoon dried chilli flakes
300 g (10 oz) baby spinach leaves
2 eggs
3 tablespoons natural yogurt
pinch of ground paprika
salt and pepper

- Heat the butter in a frying pan, add the leek and chilli flakes and cook over a medium-high heat for 4–5 minutes until softened. Add the spinach and season well, then toss and cook for 2 minutes until wilted.

- Make 2 wells in the centre of the vegetables and break the eggs into the well. Cook over a low heat for 2–3 minutes until the eggs are set. Spoon the yogurt on top and sprinkle with the paprika.

 Leek and Spinach Omelette

Heat 1 tablespoon olive oil in a large frying pan, add 1 small trimmed, cleaned and very thinly sliced leek and cook over a medium heat for 3–4 minutes, then add 175 g (6 oz) baby spinach leaves and cook for 2 minutes, stirring, until wilted. In a jug, beat together 4 eggs and season well, then pour over the spinach mixture. Cook over a low heat for 2–3 minutes until the base is set, then place a baking sheet over the top of the pan and cook for a further 1 minute until the top is set. Gently flip one side of the omelette over on to the other, then cut the omelette in half. Lightly toast 2 pieces of walnut bread and spread each with 1 tablespoon tomato chutney, then place an omelette half over each.

 Baked Spinach and Leek Frittata

Beat 5 eggs in a jug and season well. Heat 25 g (1 oz) butter in a frying pan, add 1 trimmed, cleaned and thinly sliced leek and cook over a medium heat for 3 minutes, then add 300 g (10 oz) baby spinach leaves and cook for 2 minutes, stirring continuously until wilted. Spoon into a shallow ovenproof dish and pour over the eggs. Bake in a preheated oven, 220°C (425°F), Gas Mark 7, for 20 minutes until golden and set. Serve in wedges, sprinkled with paprika.

30 Mozzarella, Tomato and Basil Thin-Crust Pizza

Serves 2

145 g (5 oz) packet pizza base mix

plain flour, for dusting

4 tablespoons sun-dried tomato paste or red pesto

1 tablespoon chopped basil leaves

1 beef tomato, sliced

150 g (5 oz) mozzarella cheese, sliced

1 tablespoon drained capers or caperberries

olive oil, for drizzling

salt and pepper

- Tip the pizza base mix into a bowl and make up according to the packet instructions. Roll out the dough on a lightly floured surface to a circle, about 25 cm (10 inches) in diameter, and place on a nonstick baking sheet.

- Place the paste or pesto in a small bowl and add the chopped basil. Spread over the pizza base, leaving a 2.5 cm (1 inch) border around the edge. Arrange the tomato and mozzarella slices over the top and scatter over the capers in the gaps between. Season well.

- Place in the top of a preheated oven, 220°C (425°F), Gas Mark 7, for 15–20 minutes until golden and cooked. Drizzle with oil and serve cut into wedges.

---

1 **Herby Mozzarella and Tomato Naan Pizza** Spread 1 large naan bread with 4 tablespoons spicy tomato chutney. Arrange 1 small sliced beef tomato and 150 g (5 oz) sliced mozzarella cheese over the top. Scatter with ½ teaspoon lightly crushed coriander seeds, then cook under a preheated hot grill for 3–4 minutes until golden and melted. Cut in half and serve scattered with 2 tablespoons chopped coriander leaves.

2 **Mozzarella, Tomato and Basil Salad with Dough Balls** Make up a 145 g (5 oz) packet pizza base mix according to the packet instructions, adding 1 tablespoon sun-dried tomato paste to the dried mix and reducing the suggested measurement water by 20 ml (1 fl oz). Mix to a smooth dough, then shape into 8 balls. Place on a nonstick baking sheet and bake in a preheated oven, 220°C (425°F), Gas Mark 7, for 12 minutes until golden and cooked through. Meanwhile, place 1 sliced beef tomato, 150 g (5 oz) thinly sliced mozzarella cheese, 1 tablespoon drained capers and 3 tablespoons shredded basil leaves in a bowl. Add 2 tablespoons olive oil, then season well and toss together. Arrange on 2 serving plates and serve with the hot dough balls.

QuickCook

Desserts

Recipes listed by cooking time

30

Fig, Raspberry and Honey Brûlées	232
Tiramisu	234
Roasted Plum and Orange Compote with Granola	236
Crushed Strawberry and Lime Shortbreads	238
Caramelized Rice Pudding with Warm Berries	240
Warm Apple Cakes with Toffee Sauce	242
Chocolate Melting Middle Puddings	244
Berry and White Chocolate Tarts	246
Lemon Polenta Cake with Vanilla Strawberries	248
Banana and Blueberry Custard Tarts	250
Pineapple Fritters with Rum Sauce	252
Filo Fruit Pies with Pistachio Yogurt	254
Chocolate Tiffin Squares	256
Tropical Fruit and Coconut Cheesecakes	258
Soft Raspberry Meringues	260

Warm Marmalade Puddings	262
Saucy Lemon and Passionfruit Pudding	264
Apple and Blackberry Compote with Almond Scones	266
Peach and Plum Clafoutis	268
Apple and Peach Marzipan Slice	270
Orange and Pistachio Polenta Muffins with Dates	272
Brioche, Banana and Maple Syrup Pudding	274
Baked Almond Peaches and Nectarines	276
Baked Chocolate Orange Mousse	278

20

Baked Honeyed Figs and Raspberries	232
Cappuccino Fudge Creams	234
Plum and Orange Fool	236
Strawberry and Lime Biscuit Stacks	238
Rice Pudding Berry Meringue	240
Pan-Fried Toffee Apples	242
Warm Chocolate Croissant Pudding	244
White Chocolate and Blackberry Turnovers	246
Lemon Eton Mess with Strawberries	248
Blueberry and Banana French Toast	250
Upside-Down Pineapple and Rum Tart	252
Grilled Fruit Parcels with Pistachio Yogurt	254
Chocolate Honeycomb Crunch	256
Coconut, Mango and Lime Layers	258
Floating Islands with Raspberries	260

10

Sticky Marmalade
Microwave Puds   262

Lemon and Passionfruit
Syllabubs   264

Fruit Compote with
Drop Scones   266

Pan-Fried Peach and
Plum Cinnamon Crunch   268

Apple and Peach
Marzipan Crumble   270

Orange Polenta Pancakes
with Dates and
Pistachios   272

Pan-Fried Banana and Maple
Syrup Brioche Rolls   274

Pan-Fried Marsala Fruit
and Almonds   276

Chilled Chocolate and
Orange Mousse   278

Fig, Raspberry and
Honey Yogurt Pots   232

Speedy Iced Tiramisu   234

Simple Pan-Fried
Orangey Plums   236

Strawberry and Lime
Brandy Snap Baskets   238

Caramelized Berry
Rice Pudding   240

Toffee Apple Pecan
Waffles   242

Chocolate Sponge
and Custard   244

Iced Berries with Hot
White Chocolate Sauce   246

Lemon Madeira and
Strawberry Trifle   248

Blueberry Pancakes
with Banana   250

Spiced Pan-Fried
Pineapple with Rum   252

Warm Fruit and
Pistachio Compote   254

Chocolate Dipped Fruits 256

Tropical Fruit Salad
with Coconut Cream   258

Mini Baked Alaskas
with Raspberries   260

Caramelized Marmalade
Oranges   262

Lemon and
Passionfruit Whips   264

Cheat's Fruit Compote
Cobbler   266

Peach and Plum
Pancakes   268

Grilled Marzipan
Peaches   270

Simple Date and
Pistachio Oranges   272

Brioche Toasts with Banana
and Maple Syrup   274

Pan-Fried Apricots
with Almonds   276

Speedy Chocolate
Orange Creams   278

Baked Honeyed Figs and Raspberries

Serves 4

8 figs, quartered
150 g (5 oz) raspberries
4 tablespoons honey
finely grated rind of 1 medium
  orange
coconut ice cream, to serve

- Cut 4 large squares of foil. Divide the figs and raspberries between the pieces of foil, drizzle over the honey and sprinkle with the orange rind.

- Bring the edges of the foil up to the centre and twist to form parcels. Place on a large baking sheet and bake in a preheated oven, 200°C (400°F), Gas Mark 6, for 15 minutes.

- Open the parcels and serve the fruit and juices with spoonfuls of coconut ice cream.

 Fig, Raspberry and Honey Yogurt Pots
Crumble 8 ginger biscuits and spoon into 4 glasses. Divide 4 chopped figs and 150 g (5 oz) raspberries between the glasses and drizzle each with honey. Spoon 3 tablespoons coconut yogurt over each and serve each topped with a raspberry.

 Fig, Raspberry and Honey Brûlées
Divide 6 chopped figs between 4 heatproof ramekins, then add 50 g (2 oz) raspberries, ½ teaspoon finely grated orange rind and ½ teaspoon honey to each. Divide 400 g (13 oz) Greek-style natural yogurt over the tops and spread evenly to cover. Place 150 g (5 oz) caster sugar in a saucepan with 1 tablespoon water and cook over a low heat, without stirring, for about 5 minutes until the sugar melts and turns a rich caramel colour. Gently tip the pan occasionally to avoid hot spots. Quickly pour the caramel over the yogurt, then leave to cool and set for 10 minutes.

1⃝ Speedy Iced Tiramisu

Serves 2

8 sponge fingers, halved
4 tablespoons strong black coffee
4 scoops of vanilla ice cream
25 g (1 oz) dark chocolate, grated

- Divide the sponge fingers between 2 serving plates or shallow bowls, then drizzle over the coffee.

- Top each with 2 scoops of the ice cream and sprinkle over the grated chocolate. Serve immediately.

2⃝ Cappuccino Fudge Creams

Mix ½ teaspoon coffee granules with 2 tablespoons boiling water, then leave to cool slightly. Beat together 175 g (6 oz) mascarpone cheese and 1 tablespoon caster sugar in a bowl. Lightly stir in the coffee and spoon the mixture into 2 glasses. Top each with a spoonful of whipped cream, then cover and chill in the refrigerator for 10 minutes. Sprinkle 25 g (1 oz) chopped fudge over the top and serve with sponge fingers.

3⃝ Tiramisu

Mix together 4 tablespoons strong black coffee and 1 tablespoon coffee liqueur in a small bowl. Place 4 sponge fingers in a shallow dish and pour over half the coffee mixture. In a separate bowl, mix together 150 g (5 oz) mascarpone cheese and 25 g (1 oz) icing sugar. Lightly whip 100 ml (3½ fl oz) double cream and fold into the mascarpone. Spoon half the mixture over the sponge fingers and spread evenly. Sift 1 teaspoon cocoa powder over the top. Repeat the layers and dust cocoa powder over the top. Cover and chill for 10 minutes.

Roasted Plum and Orange Compote with Granola

Serves 4

500 g (1 lb) plums, halved and stoned

juice and finely grated rind of 1 medium orange

75 g (3 oz) demerara sugar

½ teaspoon ground cinnamon

100 g (3½ oz) butter

50 g (2 oz) porridge oats

30 g (1 oz) hazelnuts, roughly chopped

natural yogurt, to serve

• Place the plums in a shallow roasting tin or baking dish. Add the orange rind and juice and sprinkle over 50 g (2 oz) of the sugar and the cinnamon. Dot half the butter on top and roast in a preheated oven, 200°C (400°F), Gas Mark 6, for 20 minutes, spooning over the juices halfway through, until the plums have softened.

• Meanwhile, line a large baking tray with foil, then scatter over the oats, hazelnuts and remaining sugar. Dot with the remaining butter and place in the oven with the plums for 5–10 minutes until golden and toasted, stirring once to coat in the melted butter.

• Spoon the compote into 4 serving dishes, scatter over the crunchy oat granola and serve with yogurt.

Simple Pan-Fried Orangey Plums

Heat 25 g (1 oz) butter in a frying pan, add 500 g (1 lb) halved, stoned and quartered plums and fry in the butter for 5 minutes until soft. Stir in the grated rind of 1 orange and 50 g (2 oz) demerara sugar. Sprinkle with a few roasted chopped hazelnuts and serve with custard.

Plum and Orange Fool

Place 500 g (1 lb) halved and stoned plums and the juice and grated rind of 1 orange in a saucepan and cook for 2–3 minutes. Add 50 g (2 oz) demerara sugar and 1 teaspoon ground cinnamon and cook for 5 minutes until the plums are tender. Blend with a stick bender until almost smooth, then pour into a shallow dish and leave to cool for 10 minutes. Meanwhile, whip 150 ml (¼ pint) double cream until just thick enough to form soft peaks, then fold in 2 x 150 g (5 oz) pots custard. Stir in the plum purée to create a marbled effect. Sprinkle with roasted chopped hazelnuts and serve.

30 Crushed Strawberry and Lime Shortbreads

Serves 4

100 g (3½ oz) butter
50 g (2 oz) caster sugar, plus
  1 teaspoon
150 g (5 oz) plain flour
finely grated rind of 1 lime
75 ml (3 fl oz) double cream
3 strawberries, hulled and
  chopped
icing sugar, for dusting

- Line a baking sheet with baking paper. Place the butter, 50 g (2 oz) caster sugar, flour and most of the lime rind (reserving a little for decoration) in a food processor and pulse until the mixture comes together to form a dough.

- Divide the mixture into 8 equal pieces and roll each piece into a ball. Place on the prepared baking sheet and flatten the biscuits with the back of a fork.

- Bake in a preheated oven, 180°C (350°F), Gas Mark 4, for 10–15 minutes until golden. Transfer to a wire rack to cool.

- While the biscuits are cooling, whip the cream with the remaining sugar, then fold in the strawberries.

- Sandwich together 2 biscuits with some strawberry cream, then repeat with 6 more biscuits. Decorate with lime rind and a dusting of icing sugar. Serve any remaining strawberry cream separately.

---

10 Strawberry and Lime Brandy Snap Baskets Warm 2 tablespoons strawberry jam to soften. Cool slightly, then stir in 8 hulled and sliced strawberries to coat in the jam. Place 2 tablespoons clotted cream in each of 4 shop-bought brandy snap baskets, sprinkle with a little grated lime rind and spoon the strawberries over the top.

20 Strawberry and Lime Biscuit Stacks

Whip together 200 ml (7 fl oz) double cream, the finely grated rind of 1 lime and 2 teaspoons caster sugar in a bowl. Hull and slice 150 g (5 oz) strawberries. Layer 12 shop-bought thin dessert biscuits with spoonfuls of the lime cream and the sliced strawberries to form 4 stacks of 3 biscuits each.

 # Caramelized Berry Rice Pudding

Serves 2

125 g (4 oz) frozen mixed summer berries

1 tablespoon caster sugar

425 g (14 oz) can ready-to-eat rice pudding

4 tablespoons natural yogurt

1 tablespoon soft light brown sugar

- Place the fruit in a saucepan with the caster sugar and heat, stirring, for 3–4 minutes until the fruit has softened and defrosted. Tip the fruit and juice into a flameproof dish.

- Mix together the rice pudding and yogurt in a bowl, then spoon over the fruit. Sprinkle over the brown sugar and place under a preheated hot grill for about 2 minutes until the sugar starts to melt and caramelize. Cool slightly before serving.

 ### Rice Pudding Berry Meringue

Heat 125 g (4 oz) frozen mixed summer berries with 1 tablespoon caster sugar in a saucepan for a few minutes until defrosted and juicy. Arrange 6 sponge fingers in a shallow flameproof dish and pour the warm fruit over the top. Heat 2 x 150 g (5 oz) pots ready-to-eat rice pudding in a microwave on Medium for 2 minutes until warm. Pour over the fruit. In a clean bowl, whisk 1 egg white using a hand-held electric whisk until just stiff, then add 25 g (1 oz) caster sugar, whisking well between each addition, until firm and glossy. Spoon the meringue over the rice pudding, swirling with the back of a spoon. Place under a preheated medium grill for 3–4 minutes until the meringue is golden.

 ### Caramelized Rice Pudding with

Warm Berries Gently simmer 300 ml (½ pint) milk and 25 g (1 oz) pudding rice in a saucepan for 20–25 minutes, stirring occasionally, until the milk has been absorbed and the rice is tender. Stir in 2 teaspoons caster sugar and a few drops of vanilla extract. Spoon the rice into a small flameproof dish, sprinkle over 1 tablespoon soft light brown sugar and place under a preheated hot grill for 2 minutes until the sugar melts and caramelizes. Meanwhile, heat 125 g (4 oz) frozen mixed summer berries with 1 tablespoon caster sugar in a saucepan for a few minutes until defrosted and juicy. Cool the rice pudding slightly, then serve with the warm fruit.

 # Pan-Fried Toffee Apples

Serves 4

75 g (3 oz) butter
4 dessert apples, cored and cut into wedges
75 g (3 oz) soft light brown sugar
75 ml (3 fl oz) double cream

- Heat the butter in a large frying pan, add the apple wedges and fry for 5 minutes until soft and golden. Remove from the pan and set aside.

- Add the sugar to the butter and juices in the pan and heat gently, stirring to dissolve the sugar. Simmer for 1 minute, then stir in the cream and heat through for 1 minute.

- Return the apples to the pan and coat in the toffee sauce. Cool slightly, then serve.

 Toffee Apple Pecan Waffles

Heat 25 g (1 oz) butter in a large frying pan, add 4 peeled and cored dessert apples, cut into wedges, and fry over a gentle heat for 3–4 minutes until soft and golden. Stir in 8 tablespoons ready-made toffee sauce, such as dulce de leche, and a few pecan nut halves and heat through for 1 minute. Serve on toasted waffles.

 Warm Apple Cakes with Toffee Sauce

Place 50 g (2 oz) self-raising flour, 50 g (2 oz) soft light brown sugar, 50 g (2 oz) soft margarine and 1 egg in a food processor. Blend until soft and smooth. Stir in ½ peeled, cored and chopped dessert apple. Spoon the mixture into 4 holes of a muffin tin lined with paper muffin cases. Bake in a preheated oven, 180°C (350°F),

Gas Mark 4, for 15 minutes until risen and firm to the touch. Meanwhile, melt 50 g (2 oz) butter and 50 g (2 oz) soft light brown sugar in a saucepan. Bring to the boil, then stir in 150 ml (¼ pint) double cream. Simmer and stir to make a smooth toffee sauce. Remove the cakes from the paper cases and serve with the slightly cooled toffee sauce.

30 Chocolate Melting Middle Puddings

Serves 2

75 g (3 oz) butter, plus extra for greasing

75 g (3 oz) caster sugar

75 g (3 oz) plain chocolate, broken into pieces

2 small eggs

25 g (1 oz) plain flour

To serve

cream

raspberries

- Grease 2 individual ovenproof pudding basins or ramekins and sprinkle with 1 teaspoon of the sugar.

- Melt together the chocolate and butter in a microwaveable bowl in a microwave on Medium, checking every minute until melted and smooth.

- Whisk together the eggs and remaining sugar with a hand-held electric whisk until very thick, pale and creamy. Whisk in the melted chocolate mixture, then lightly fold in the flour.

- Spoon the mixture into the prepared basins or ramekins and place on a baking sheet. Bake in a preheated oven, 190 °C (375 °F), Gas Mark 5, for 15–20 minutes until firm on the outside but still wobbly in the centre.

- Turn out the puddings into 2 serving bowls and serve warm with cream and raspberries.

1 Chocolate Sponge and Custard

Heat a 150 g (5 oz) pot custard in a small saucepan, then stir in 1 tablespoon chocolate hazelnut spread. Warm 2 chocolate muffins in a microwave on Medium for 30 seconds, then serve with the chocolate custard spooned over.

2 Warm Chocolate Croissant Pudding

Split 2 croissants and spread each with 1 tablespoon chocolate spread. Cut into thick slices and place in a shallow ovenproof dish. Beat together 1 egg, 150 ml (¼ pint) milk and 1 tablespoon caster sugar in a jug, then pour over the croissants. Bake in a preheated oven, 190 °C (375 °F), Gas Mark 5, for 15 minutes until the custard has just set. Sprinkle with 1 crumbled chocolate flake and serve with cream.

30 Berry and White Chocolate Tarts

Serves 2

½ x 375 g (12 oz) pack ready-made sweet pastry

plain flour, for dusting

50 g (2 oz) white chocolate, broken into pieces

75 g (3 oz) mascarpone cheese

2 tablespoons single cream

75 g (3 oz) mixed blackberries and raspberries

white chocolate shavings, to decorate

icing sugar, for dusting

- Roll out the pastry on a lightly floured surface, then cut out 2 circles and use to line 2 x 10 cm (4 inch) tart tins, trimming off any excess. Prick the bases with a fork and line with baking paper and baking beans.

- Place the tins on a baking sheet and bake in a preheated oven, 190°C (375°F), Gas Mark 5, for 10 minutes. Remove the paper and beans and return to the oven for a further 5 minutes until the pastry is crisp and golden. Leave to cool.

- Meanwhile, melt the white chocolate in a microwaveable bowl in a microwave on Medium, checking every 30 seconds until melted and smooth, taking care not to let it overheat.

- Beat together the mascarpone and cream in a bowl until smooth, then beat in the melted chocolate. Spoon the mixture into the cases, then top with the fruit and some white chocolate shavings. Dust with icing sugar and serve.

10 Iced Berries with Hot White Chocolate Sauce

Place 150 g (5 oz) frozen mixed summer berries on a microwaveable plate, then place in a microwave on Defrost for 1 minute until just starting to soften. Divide between 2 glasses or dishes. Melt together 75 g (3 oz) chopped white chocolate, broken into pieces, and 100 ml (3½ fl oz) double cream in a microwaveable bowl in a microwave on Medium, checking every 30 seconds until melted and smooth. Pour the warm sauce over the fruit and serve immediately.

20 White Chocolate and Blackberry Turnovers

Cut ½ x 375 g (12 oz) sheet of ready-rolled puff pastry into 2 x 15 cm (6 inch) squares. Divide 75 g (3 oz) blackberries and 50 g (2 oz) chopped white chocolate between the squares. Brush the edges with a little beaten egg and fold the pastry over the filling to make triangles. Press the edges firmly with the back of a fork to seal. Place the turnovers on a baking sheet, brush with beaten egg and sprinkle with a little caster sugar. Bake in a preheated oven, 200°C (400°F), Gas Mark 6, for 15 minutes until well risen and golden.

30 Lemon Polenta Cake with Vanilla Strawberries

Serves 4

75 g (3 oz) butter, softened, plus extra for greasing

150 g (5 oz) caster sugar

1 egg

75 g (3 oz) ricotta cheese

25 g (1 oz) ground almonds

25 g (1 oz) polenta (cornmeal)

½ teaspoon baking powder

grated rind of 1 lemon

50 ml (2 fl oz) water

½ teaspoon vanilla bean paste or extract

75 g (3 oz) strawberries, hulled and halved

- Grease a 15 cm (6 inch) sandwich cake tin and line the base with baking paper. In a bowl, beat together the butter, 75 g (3 oz) of the sugar, the egg, ricotta, ground almonds, polenta, baking powder and lemon rind using a hand-held electric whisk until smooth.

- Spoon the mixture into the prepared tin and level the surface. Bake in a preheated oven, 190°C (375°F), Gas Mark 5, for 20 minutes until golden and firm to the touch.

- Meanwhile, place the remaining sugar in a saucepan with the measurement water and heat, stirring, to dissolve the sugar. Simmer for 3 minutes until syrupy. Cool slightly, then stir in the vanilla bean paste or extract.

- Remove the cake from the tin and cut into wedges (any extra cake can be frozen). Mix the strawberries with the vanilla syrup and spoon over the cake to serve.

 Lemon Madeira and Strawberry Trifle

Spread 4 slices of shop-bought Madeira cake with 2 tablespoons lemon curd. Cut into cubes and place in a dish or 4 glasses with 8 hulled and chopped strawberries. Mix together a 300 g (10 oz) pot custard and 2 tablespoons lemon curd in a separate bowl, then spoon over the cake and strawberries. Top with 4 tablespoons extra thick double cream. Sprinkle over a few chopped pistachio nuts and serve.

 Lemon Eton Mess with Strawberries

Lightly whip 300 ml (10 fl oz) double cream in a bowl until just thick enough to form soft peaks. Break 4 meringue nests into pieces and add to the bowl with 100 g (3½ oz) hulled and chopped strawberries. Lightly fold into the cream with 2 tablespoons lemon curd. Spoon into 4 glasses and top each with 1 teaspoon lemon curd and ½ hulled strawberry.

Blueberry and Banana French Toast

Serves 4

2 eggs
4 tablespoons milk
4 teaspoons caster sugar
4 slices of crusty white bread
50 g (2 oz) butter
50 g (2 oz) blueberries
2 bananas, sliced

To serve

ice cream
maple syrup

- Beat together the eggs, milk and 2 teaspoons of the caster sugar in a jug. Pour into a shallow dish and dip both sides of the bread slices into the egg mixture.

- Heat the butter in a large frying pan, add the bread (you might need to cook 1 slice at a time) and cook for 2 minutes on each side until crisp and golden. Sprinkle over the remaining sugar.

- Cut the French toasts in half diagonally and scatter with the blueberries and banana slices. Serve with ice cream and a drizzle of maple syrup.

 Blueberry Pancakes with Banana

Place 75 g (3 oz) self-raising flour, 1 tablespoon caster sugar, 1 egg and 75 ml (3 fl oz) milk in a food processor or blender and blitz together to make a smooth, thick batter. Stir in 25 g (1 oz) blueberries. Heat 1 tablespoon sunflower oil in a large frying pan, add 2 large spoonfuls of the batter and cook for 1–2 minutes on each side until golden. Repeat with the remaining batter to make another 2 pancakes. Serve warm with sliced banana and a drizzle of honey.

 Banana and Blueberry Custard Tarts Unroll a 375 g (12 oz) sheet of ready-rolled shortcrust pastry and cut out circles large enough to line 4 x 10 cm (4 inch) tart tins or Yorkshire pudding tins. Slice 1 large banana and place the slices over the pastry bases with a few blueberries. Beat together 2 eggs, 125 ml (4 fl oz) single cream and 2 tablespoons caster sugar in a jug, then pour into the pastry cases. Bake in a preheated oven, 190°C (375°F), Gas Mark 5, for 20 minutes until the pastry is cooked and the filling is just set. Dust with icing sugar and serve with a few extra blueberries.

Spiced Pan-Fried Pineapple with Rum

Serves 2

25 g (1 oz) butter

4 ready-prepared fresh pineapple wedges, skin removed, or canned slices

50 g (2 oz) soft light brown sugar

1 piece of stem ginger from a jar, chopped

2 tablespoons stem ginger syrup from the jar

2 tablespoons raisins

50 ml (2 fl oz) rum

coconut ice cream, to serve

- Heat the butter in a frying pan, add the pineapple and cook over a high heat for 2 minutes until starting to brown. Reduce the heat, add the sugar, ginger, ginger syrup and raisins and simmer for 1 minute until the sugar has dissolved.

- Add the rum and cook for 2 minutes until the sauce is syrupy. Serve warm with scoops of coconut ice cream.

 Upside-Down Pineapple and Rum Tart Heat 4 tablespoons ready-made toffee sauce in an ovenproof 15 cm (6 inch) frying pan. Add a dash of rum and stir well. Cut 3 drained canned pineapple slices in half, place in the pan in a single layer and heat through. Unroll a 375 g (12 oz) sheet of ready-rolled puff pastry and cut out a 20 cm (8 inch) circle. Remove the pan from the heat and place the pastry over the fruit, tucking in the edges. Place in a preheated oven, 200°C (400°F), Gas Mark 6, for 15 minutes until golden and well risen. Turn out on to a plate, taking care as the juices will be hot. Serve warm with ice cream.

 Pineapple Fritters with Rum Sauce Heat 25 g (1 oz) butter and 50 g (2 oz) soft light brown sugar in a saucepan, stirring to dissolve the sugar. Drain a 227 g (7½ oz) can pineapple slices, reserving the juice, then add 3 tablespoons of the juice to the pan and simmer for 2 minutes. Add a splash of rum and remove from the heat. Whisk together 75 g (3 oz) plain flour, 1 egg plus 1 egg yolk and 75 ml (3 fl oz) milk in a bowl to make a batter. In a clean bowl, whisk 1 egg white until just stiff, then fold into the batter. Pat the pineapple slices dry on kitchen paper, then dip in the batter, one at a time, to coat. Heat about 2.5 cm (1 inch) vegetable oil in a large frying pan until hot, then fry the pineapple slices for a few minutes until crisp and golden. Remove with a slotted spoon and place on a plate with 25 g (1 oz) caster sugar mixed with a large pinch of ground cinnamon. Turn the fritters in the sugar to coat. Warm the rum sauce and serve with the fritters.

Grilled Fruit Parcels with Pistachio Yogurt

Serves 2

125 g (4 oz) mixed blueberries and raspberries

2 peaches or nectarines, halved, stoned and sliced

½ cinnamon stick, halved

1 tablespoon clear honey

2 tablespoons orange juice

25 g (1 oz) shelled pistachio nuts, chopped, plus extra to decorate

4 tablespoons Greek-style natural yogurt

- Cut 2 large, double thickness squares of foil. Divide the fruit and cinnamon between the squares and drizzle over the honey and orange juice. Fold the foil over the filling and scrunch the edges to seal.

- Place the parcels under a preheated medium grill or on a barbecue for about 10 minutes until the fruit is soft and hot.

- Open the parcels and transfer the fruit to serving bowls. Mix together the pistachios and yogurt in a bowl. Serve with an extra sprinkling of pistachios and spoon the yogurt over the warm fruit.

 Warm Fruit and Pistachio Compote

Place 125 g (4 oz) mixed blueberries and raspberries, 1 halved, stoned and chopped peach, 1 tablespoon clear honey, 2 tablespoons orange juice and ½ cinnamon stick in a saucepan, then simmer gently for 5 minutes. Sprinkle with chopped pistachio nuts and serve with amaretti biscuits and thick Greek yogurt.

 Filo Fruit Pies with Pistachio Yogurt

Cut 2 sheets of filo pastry into 6 x 15 cm (6 inch) squares. Melt 25 g (1 oz) butter and brush some of it over each square. Place 3 squares on top of each other to make 2 stacks. Divide 1 halved, stoned and chopped peach, 25 g (1 oz) blueberries and 25 g (1 oz) raspberries between the squares, then sprinkle with a pinch of ground cinnamon and the grated rind of ½ orange. Gather the filo pastry up over the filling and scrunch at the top to secure. Place on a baking sheet and brush with the remaining melted butter. Bake in a preheated oven, 190°C (375°F), Gas Mark 5, for 20 minutes until crisp and golden. Stir 25 g (1 oz) chopped pistachio nuts into 4 tablespoons natural yogurt in a bowl. Serve with the warm pies with a drizzle of honey.

Chocolate Tiffin Squares

Makes 8

50 g (2 oz) butter, plus extra for greasing

200 g (7 oz) plain chocolate, broken into pieces

1½ tablespoons golden syrup

75 g (3 oz) digestive biscuits, roughly crushed

25 g (1 oz) ready-to-eat dried apricots, chopped

25 g (1 oz) glâcé cherries, chopped

2 tablespoons desiccated coconut

· Grease a 15 x 15 cm (6 x 6 inch) baking tin. Gently heat the butter, 150 g (5 oz) of the chocolate and the golden syrup in a saucepan until melted and smooth. Stir in the crushed biscuits, apricots, cherries and coconut until evenly coated in the chocolate. Tip the mixture into the prepared tin and roughly spread level.

· Melt the remaining chocolate in a microwaveable bowl in a microwave on Medium, checking every 30 seconds until melted and smooth. Drizzle over the biscuit mixture. Cover and chill in the freezer for 15 minutes until firm.

· Cut into 8 squares and serve with coffee.

Chocolate Dipped Fruits

Melt 75 g (3 oz) plain chocolate, broken into pieces, in a small microwaveable bowl in a microwave on Medium, checking every 30 seconds until melted and smooth. Dip a selection of fruit, such as strawberries, cherries and ready-to-eat dried apricots, in the chocolate and place on a baking sheet lined with baking paper. Chill in the refrigerator for 5 minutes to set.

Chocolate Honeycomb Crunch

Melt 25 g (1 oz) butter in a small saucepan and stir in 50 g (2 oz) crushed chocolate digestive biscuits. Spoon into the bases of 2 ramekins and press down firmly with the back of a spoon. Melt together 1 tablespoon clear honey and 100 g (3½ oz) plain chocolate, broken into pieces, in a microwaveable bowl in a microwave on Medium, checking every 30 seconds until melted

and smooth. Stir in 125 g (4 oz) mascarpone cheese and spoon over the biscuit bases. Cover and chill in the freezer for 10 minutes. Serve sprinkled with 1 chopped mini chocolate honeycomb bar.

30 Tropical Fruit and Coconut Cheesecakes

Serves 2

25 g (1 oz) butter

75 g (3 oz) coconut biscuits, crushed

125 g (4 oz) full-fat soft cheese

3 tablespoons condensed milk

finely grated rind and juice of 1 lime

2 tablespoons diced pineapple and mango

- Melt the butter in a small saucepan and stir in the crushed biscuits. Divide between 2 dessert glasses and press down with the back of a spoon.

- Mix together the soft cheese, condensed milk, most of the lime rind (reserving a little for decoration) and the lime juice in a bowl. Spoon over the biscuit bases and spread evenly. Cover and chill in the fridge for 10 minutes.

- Top with the tropical fruits and reserved lime rind and serve.

 Tropical Fruit Salad with Coconut Cream Place 250 g (8 oz) ready-prepared tropical fruits, ½ piece of stem ginger, sliced, and 2 tablespoons stem ginger syrup from the jar in a bowl and stir well to coat the fruit in the syrup. Mix together 4 tablespoons crème fraîche, a pinch of ground ginger and 1 teaspoon desiccated coconut in a separate bowl, mix well and serve with the fruit salad.

 Coconut, Mango and Lime Layers Crush 75 g (3 oz) coconut biscuits and divide half between 2 glasses. In a bowl, blend 1 peeled, stoned and chopped mango with a stick blender until smooth. Add most of the grated rind (reserving a little for decoration) and all the juice of 1 lime and stir to mix. Beat together 75 g (3 oz) full-fat soft cheese and 50 g (2 oz) condensed milk in a separate bowl until soft, then fold in the mango purée. Spoon half the mango mixture on to the biscuits, then repeat the layers. Sprinkle with the reserved lime rind and serve.

30 Soft Raspberry Meringues

Serves 4

2 egg whites

100 g (3½ oz) caster sugar

50 g (2 oz) raspberries, plus extra to serve

crème fraîche, to serve

- Line a large baking sheet with baking paper. In a clean bowl, whisk the egg whites using a hand-held electric whisk until stiff. Add the sugar, 1 tablespoon at a time, whisking well between each addition, until firm and glossy.

- Place the raspberries in a bowl and crush with a fork, then lightly fold through the meringue to form a rippled effect. Place large spoonfuls of the mixture on the prepared baking sheet.

- Bake in a preheated oven, 180°C (350°F), Gas Mark 4, for 20 minutes until firm on the outside. Serve with crème fraîche and extra raspberries.

 Mini Baked Alaskas with Raspberries

Place 4 digestive biscuits on a baking sheet lined with baking paper and top each with 1 scoop of strawberry ice cream. Place in the freezer. In a clean bowl, whisk 4 egg whites using a hand-held electric whisk until stiff. Add 200 g (7 oz) caster sugar, 1 tablespoon at a time, whisking well between each addition, until firm and glossy. Quickly spoon the meringue over the ice cream and biscuits, making sure they are completely covered. Place in a preheated oven, 220°C (425°F), Gas Mark 7, for 2–3 minutes until the meringue is golden. Serve immediately, while the ice cream is still frozen, scattered with fresh raspberries.

 Floating Islands with Raspberries

In a clean bowl, whisk 2 egg whites using a hand-held electric whisk until stiff. Add 100 g (3½ oz) caster sugar, 1 tablespoon at a time, whisking well between each addition, until firm and glossy. Poach spoonfuls of the meringue in a saucepan of simmering water for 2–3 minutes until firm. Drain with a slotted spoon. Pour a little warmed custard over the bases of 4 serving bowls, scatter over some fresh raspberries and place the poached meringues on top.

MID-DESS-KEK

30 Warm Marmalade Puddings

Serves 4

125 g (4 oz) sunflower spread, plus extra for greasing
125 g (4 oz) self-raising flour
125 g (4 oz) soft light brown sugar
2 eggs
4 tablespoons marmalade
2 tablespoons orange juice
12 tablespoons Grand Marnier
strips of orange rind, to decorate
crème fraîche, to serve

- Grease an 18 cm (7 inch) sandwich cake tin and line the base with baking paper. Place the flour, sugar, sunflower spread and eggs in a food processor and blend until soft and smooth. Spoon into the prepared tin and bake in a preheated oven, 180°C (350°F), Gas Mark 4, for 20–25 minutes until golden and firm to the touch.

- Meanwhile, place the marmalade, orange juice and Grand Marnier in a small saucepan and simmer for a few minutes to make a syrupy sauce.

- Break the cake into pieces, then stack a few pieces in 4 shallow bowls and spoon over the marmalade sauce.

- Serve with crème fraîche and sprinkled with strips of orange rind to decorate.

 Caramelized Marmalade Oranges Using a serrated knife, remove the peel and pith from 4 oranges, then cut into thick slices and arrange on 4 serving plates. Heat 4 tablespoons marmalade, 2 tablespoons orange juice and 2 tablespoons Grand Marnier in a small saucepan, then simmer for a few minutes until syrupy. Pour over the oranges and sprinkle with toasted flaked almonds.

 Sticky Marmalade Microwave Puds Beat together 150 g (5 oz) sunflower spread, 150 g (5 oz) self-raising flour, 150 g (5 oz) soft light brown sugar, 2 large eggs and 2 tablespoons marmalade in a food processor or with a hand-held electric whisk until smooth and creamy. Add a little milk if the mixture is too stiff. Place 1 teaspoon marmalade in each of 4 greased microwaveable individual pudding basins or dishes. Spoon the sponge mixture over the top and cook in a microwave on Medium for 5 minutes. Leave to stand for 5 minutes, then turn out and serve with custard.

 # Lemon and Passionfruit Whips

Serves 2

50 g (2 oz) shortbread biscuits, crushed

150 ml (¼ pint) double cream

120 g (4 oz) pot lemon yogurt

2 passionfruit, halved

- Divide the crushed biscuits between 2 glasses. Whip the cream in a bowl until just thick enough to form soft peaks, then lightly fold in the yogurt with the seeds and pulp from 1 of the passionfruit.

- Spoon the mixture into the glasses and spoon the remaining passionfruit seeds and pulp over the top.

 Lemon and Passionfruit Syllabubs Divide the seeds and pulp from 1 halved passionfruit between 2 glasses. Using a hand-held electric whisk, whisk together 150 ml (¼ pint) double cream, 3 tablespoons medium-dry white wine, 40 g (1½ oz) caster sugar, the finely grated rind of ½ lemon and the seeds and pulp from 1 halved passionfruit in a bowl until the mixture is thick enough to form soft peaks when the whisk is lifted. Spoon into the glasses, cover and chill for 5–10 minutes. Serve with shortbread biscuits.

 Saucy Lemon and Passionfruit Pudding Whisk 2 egg yolks, 50 g (2 oz) caster sugar and 100 ml (3½ fl oz) milk in a bowl until smooth. Stir in 15 g (½ oz) plain flour, the grated rind and juice of ½ lemon and the pulp and seeds of 1 passionfruit. In a clean bowl, whisk 2 egg whites using a hand-held electric whisk until stiff, then fold into the lemon mixture. Pour into a greased 600 ml (1 pint) baking dish and place in a roasting tin. Pour boiling water into the tin to come halfway up the side of the dish. Bake in a preheated oven, 180°C (350°F), Gas Mark 4, for 20 minutes until just golden. Dust with icing sugar and serve immediately, with the sauce that has formed in the bottom of the dish.

30 Apple and Blackberry Compote with Almond Scones

Serves 4

400 g (13 oz) Bramley apples, peeled, cored and sliced

2 tablespoons water

150 g (5 oz) blackberries

2 tablespoons apricot jam

clotted cream, to serve

For the scones

125 g (4 oz) self-raising flour, plus extra for dusting

50 g (2 oz) ground almonds

75 g (3 oz) caster sugar

50 g (2 oz) butter

6 tablespoons milk, plus extra for brushing

1 teaspoon vanilla extract

30 g (1 oz) flaked almonds

- To make the scones, place the flour, ground almonds, sugar and butter in a food processor and pulse to make fine crumbs. Add the milk and vanilla extract and pulse to make a soft dough. Turn out the dough on to a floured surface and lightly knead. Press the mixture out with your fingers, then stamp out 8 rounds using a 7 cm (3 inch) cutter.

- Place the scones on a baking sheet, brush with a little milk and sprinkle with the flaked almonds. Bake in a preheated oven, 200°C (400°F), Gas Mark 6, for 10–15 minutes until golden.

- Meanwhile, place the apples in a saucepan with the measurement water and cook for 3 minutes until soft. Stir in the blackberries and apricot jam and simmer for 1 minute.

- Spoon the compote into 4 shallow bowls, top each with 2 scones and serve with clotted cream.

 Cheat's Fruit Compote Cobbler

Warm a 450 g (14½ oz) pot apple and berry fruit compote in a saucepan for 2 minutes, then tip into a baking dish. Break 2 shop-bought ready-made scones into chunks and scatter over the fruit. Sprinkle with 4 teaspoons demerara sugar and 2 tablespoons flaked almonds and bake in a preheated oven, 200°C (400°F), Gas Mark 6, for 5 minutes until hot. Serve with clotted cream.

20 Fruit Compote with Drop Scones

Mix together 150 g (5 oz) self-raising flour, a large pinch of salt and 4 teaspoons caster sugar in a bowl. Make a well in the centre, then add 1 large egg. Gradually add 150 ml (¼ pint) milk, whisking continuously to make a smooth, thick batter. Heat a little butter in a large frying pan, add spoonfuls of the batter and cook until set and golden underneath. Turn the scones over and cook for a further 30 seconds. Repeat with the remaining batter to make about 8 scones. Meanwhile, place 350 g (11½ oz) peeled, cored and chopped Bramley apples in a saucepan with 50 g (2 oz) caster sugar and 4 tablespoons water. Simmer for 3 minutes until soft, then stir in 150 g (5 oz) blackberries and cook for 1 minute. Sprinkle the scones with flaked almonds and serve warm with the fruit compote.

Pan-Fried Peach and Plum Cinnamon Crunch

Serves 4

75 g (3 oz) butter

4 peaches, halved, stoned and cut into wedges

6 plums, halved and stoned

4 tablespoons soft light brown sugar

1 teaspoon ground cinnamon

4 digestive biscuits, crushed

ice cream, to serve

- Heat half the butter in a large, flameproof frying pan, add the peaches, plums and sugar and simmer gently for 5 minutes, turning occasionally, until soft.

- In a separate saucepan, melt the remaining butter and stir in the cinnamon. Add the crushed biscuits and stir to coat. Sprinkle over the peaches and plums.

- Place the frying pan under a preheated medium grill and cook for 5 minutes until golden and crunchy. Serve with ice cream.

Peach and Plum Pancakes

Heat 50 g (2 oz) butter in a frying pan, add 2 halved, stoned and sliced peaches, 6 halved, stoned and chopped plums, 4 tablespoons caster sugar and 1 teaspoon ground cinnamon and cook for 5 minutes until the fruit is soft and the juices syrupy. Warm 8 Scotch pancakes in the toaster or under a preheated grill, then serve with the warm fruit and spoonfuls of crème fraîche.

Peach and Plum Clafoutis

Place 2 halved, stoned and sliced peaches and 4 halved, stoned and chopped plums in a greased shallow 1.2 litre (2 pint) baking dish. Place 4 eggs, 100 g (3½ oz) caster sugar, 75 g (3 oz) plain flour, 1 teaspoon ground cinnamon, 600 ml (1 pint) milk and 50 g (2 oz) melted butter in a food processor or blender and blend to make a smooth batter. Pour over the fruit and bake in a preheated oven, 190 °C (375 °F),

Gas Mark 5, for 25 minutes until golden and set. Serve dusted with icing sugar.

30 Apple and Peach Marzipan Slice

Serves 2

½ x 375 g (12 oz) sheet of ready-rolled puff pastry

1 dessert apple, peeled, cored and coarsely grated

1 peach, halved, stoned and chopped

25 g (1 oz) coarsely grated marzipan

beaten egg, to glaze

2 teaspoons caster sugar

icing sugar, for dusting

custard, to serve

- Place the pastry on a baking sheet and add the apple down one side. Top with the peach and scatter over the marzipan.

- Brush the edge of the pastry with a little beaten egg, fold the pastry over the filling and press the edges with the back of a fork to seal. Cut a few slashes across the top of the pastry, brush with beaten egg and sprinkle with the caster sugar.

- Bake in a preheated oven, 200°C (400°F), Gas Mark 6, for 20 minutes until crisp and golden. Dust with icing sugar, then slice and serve with custard.

 Grilled Marzipan Peaches

Place 2 halved and stoned peaches, cut side up, in a small, shallow flameproof dish. Mix together 25 g (1 oz) chopped marzipan and 2 crushed digestive biscuits in a bowl, then spoon over the peaches. Drizzle with honey and cook under a preheated medium grill for 5 minutes until soft and the marzipan is melted and bubbling. Sprinkle over a few chopped pecan nuts and serve with cream.

 Apple and Peach Marzipan Crumble

Place 1 peeled, cored and chopped apple with 1 tablespoon water in a saucepan and cook for 3 minutes until soft. Stir in 1 halved, stoned and chopped peach and 2 tablespoons apricot jam. Tip the mixture into a small ovenproof dish. Meanwhile, melt 25 g (1 oz) butter in a separate saucepan, add 1 tablespoon golden syrup, 50 g (2 oz) porridge oats, 25 g (1 oz) chopped marzipan and

1 tablespoon chopped pecan nuts and mix well. Sprinkle the mixture over the fruit and bake in a preheated oven, 190°C (375°F), Gas Mark 5, for 10 minutes until crisp. Serve with custard.

30 Orange and Pistachio Polenta Muffins with Dates

Serves 2

50 g (2 oz) plain flour
50 g (2 oz) polenta (cornmeal)
50 g (2 oz) caster sugar, plus
  2 tablespoons
½ teaspoon baking powder
1 egg, beaten
25 g (1 oz) butter, melted
grated rind and juice of 1 orange
2 tablespoons shelled pistachio
  nuts, roughly chopped
25 g (1 oz) fresh dates, pitted and
  roughly chopped

- Line 4 holes of a muffin tin with paper muffin cases. Sift the flour into a bowl, then add the polenta, the 50 g (2 oz) caster sugar and the baking powder. In a jug, mix together the egg, melted butter and orange rind, then pour into the dry ingredients and stir until just combined. Add 1 tablespoon of the pistachios.

- Spoon the mixture into the prepared muffin tin and bake in a preheated oven, 180°C (350°F), Gas Mark 4, for 15–20 minutes until golden, risen and cooked through.

- Meanwhile, place the orange juice and remaining sugar in a saucepan and bring to the boil, then reduce the heat and simmer for 2 minutes until syrupy.

- Remove the muffins from the oven and pierce each 3–4 times with a skewer, then pour 1 tablespoon of the syrup over each. Serve scattered with the roughly chopped dates and remaining pistachios.

 Simple Date and Pistachio Oranges
Using a serrated knife, remove the peel and pith from 3 oranges, then cut into slices. Place in a bowl with 6 pitted and roughly chopped fresh dates, 2 tablespoons clear honey and 2 tablespoons roughly chopped pistachio nuts. Serve with ice cream or crème fraîche.

 Orange Polenta Pancakes with Dates and Pistachios Place 75 g (3 oz) polenta (cornmeal), 1 tablespoon plain flour and ½ teaspoon baking powder in a bowl. Add 1 beaten egg and the finely grated rind and juice of 1 orange and mix well. Heat a little butter in a frying pan, add large tablespoons of the mixture, well spaced apart, and cook for 1 minute, then flip over using a palette knife and cook for about 1 minute until pale golden. Repeat with the remaining batter to make 6 pancakes. Serve drizzled with honey and scattered with 2 tablespoons pitted and roughly chopped fresh dates and 2 tablespoons roughly chopped pistachio nuts.

Pan-Fried Banana and Maple Syrup Brioche Rolls

Serves 2

2 eggs, beaten
8 tablespoons milk
1 teaspoon vanilla extract
½ teaspoon ground cinnamon
4 thin slices of brioche
1 ripe banana
1 tablespoon maple syrup, plus extra to drizzle
25 g (1 oz) butter
vanilla yogurt, to serve

- Beat together the eggs, milk, vanilla extract and cinnamon in a shallow dish until well blended. Place the brioche slices in the egg mixture and leave to soak for 2 minutes.

- Mash together the banana and maple syrup in a separate bowl. Carefully remove the slices of brioche from the egg mixture and place on a board. Divide the banana mixture between the slices and spread to within the edges. Roll up and secure each with a cocktail stick.

- Heat the butter in a frying pan. Using a fish slice, carefully place each roll in the pan and cook for 4–5 minutes until golden, turning halfway through cooking. Serve hot with spoonfuls of vanilla yogurt and drizzled with maple syrup.

 Brioche Toasts with Banana and Maple Syrup Beat together 1 egg, 5 tablespoons milk and ½ teaspoon vanilla extract in a shallow dish. Dip 2 slices of brioche into the mixture. Heat 25 g (1 oz) butter in a frying pan, add the brioche slices and cook for 2 minutes on each side until golden. Slice 1 banana and arrange on top of each, then drizzle over maple syrup. Serve with spoonfuls of vanilla yogurt.

Brioche, Banana and Maple Syrup Pudding Lightly butter 4 slices of brioche, then cut in half diagonally. Toss 1 thinly sliced banana with 2 tablespoons maple syrup in a bowl. In a small, shallow ovenproof dish, layer the brioche slices with the bananas. Beat together 2 eggs, 150 ml (¼ pint) milk and 1 teaspoon vanilla extract in a jug. Slowly pour over the brioche, allowing the bread to soak up the milk mixture. Bake in the top of a preheated oven, 200°C (400°F), Gas Mark 6, for 20 minutes until golden and just firm. Serve hot with vanilla yogurt.

Pan-Fried Marsala Fruit and Almonds

Serves 2

25 g (1 oz) unsalted butter

1 peach, halved, stoned and quartered

1 nectarine, halved, stoned and quartered

4 apricots, halved and stoned

2 tablespoons soft brown sugar

2 tablespoons marsala

1 tablespoon clear honey

3 tablespoons toasted flaked almonds

vanilla ice cream, to serve

- Heat the butter in a frying pan, add the fruit and cook over a medium-high heat for 3–4 minutes until softened and golden in places, turning once or twice.

- Add the sugar and cook, gently tossing, for a further 1 minute, then add the marsala. Heat, stirring, for 1 minute, then add the honey and almonds and stir to coat. Serve with scoops of vanilla ice cream.

Pan-Fried Apricots with Almonds

Heat 25 g (1 oz) butter in a frying pan, add 8 halved and stoned apricots and cook over a medium heat, cut side down, for 2–3 minutes. Scatter over 3 tablespoons soft brown sugar and 1 tablespoon clear honey and cook over a low heat for a further 2–3 minutes, turning occasionally. Sprinkle with 1 tablespoon toasted flaked almonds and serve hot with ice cream or crème fraîche.

Baked Almond Peaches and Nectarines

Halve and stone 2 peaches and 2 nectarines and place in a shallow ovenproof dish. Place 25 g (1 oz) butter and 2 tablespoons soft brown sugar in a saucepan and gently stir and heat until smooth and syrupy. Add 1 tablespoon marsala and stir again until smooth, then drizzle over the peaches. Grate 50 g (2 oz) marzipan and sprinkle over the fruit, then scatter with 25 g (1 oz) flaked almonds. Bake in a preheated oven, 180°C (350°F), Gas Mark 4, for 20 minutes until soft and golden in places. Serve with crème fraîche, if liked.

30 Baked Chocolate Orange Mousse

Serves 4

200 g (7 oz) milk chocolate,
    broken into pieces
100 g (3½ oz) butter
2 eggs
40 g (1½ oz) caster sugar,
finely grated rind of 1 orange, plus
    extra pared rind to decorate
icing sugar, for dusting

- Melt the chocolate and butter in a heatproof bowl set over a saucepan of gently simmering water, making sure the base of the bowl does not touch the water. Leave to cool slightly.

- Combine the eggs and sugar in a bowl and whisk together using a hand-held electric whisk until thick. Carefully fold in the orange rind, then the melted chocolate mixture.

- Spoon the mixture into 4 large ramekins and bake in a preheated oven, 180°C (350°F), Gas Mark 4, for 15 minutes until the tops are just set.

- Leave to cool for 2 minutes, then scatter with the pared orange rind. Serve warm dusted with a little icing sugar.

1 Speedy Chocolate Orange Creams

Melt together 200 g (7 oz) milk chocolate, broken into pieces, and 175 ml (6 fl oz) double cream in a heatproof bowl set over a saucepan of gently simmering water, stirring until smooth and melted. Leave to cool slightly. Lightly crush a 100 g (3½ oz) bar orange chocolate and divide between 4 glasses. Pour over the chocolate cream and chill for 5 minutes before serving.

2 Chilled Chocolate and Orange Mousse

Melt 150 g (5 oz) milk chocolate, broken into pieces, in a heatproof bowl set over a saucepan of gently simmering water, then leave to cool slightly. Add 4 egg yolks and stir well. In a clean bowl, whisk 4 egg whites with a hand-held electric whisk until stiff, then gently fold into the chocolate mixture with the finely grated rind of 1 orange. Divide between 4 glasses and chill for at least 5 minutes before serving.

Index

Page references in *italics* indicate photographs

anchovies
anchovy tomato toasts 138
baked anchovy tomatoes with spaghetti 138, *139*
spaghetti puttanesca 138
apples
apple and blackberry compote with almond scones 266, *267*
apple and peach marzipan slice *19*, 270, *271*
creamy pork, apple and mustard pan-fry *12*, 54, *55*
pan-fried toffee apples 242
pork, apple and mustard gratins 54
simple pork, apple and mustard pan-fry 54
toffee apple pecan waffles 242
warm apple cakes with toffee sauce 242
apricots
pan-fried apricots with almonds 276
artichokes
chicken, artichoke and olive pan-fry 100
chicken, artichoke and olive pasta 100
chickpea, artichoke and tomato pan-fry *17*, 202, *203*
Greek chicken stifado *14*, 100, *101*
pepperoni, artichoke and olive crostini 34
pepperoni, artichoke and olive pizzas *14*, 34, *35*
pepperoni, artichoke and olive tart 34
warm chickpea, artichoke and tomato stew 202
asparagus
asparagus, aubergine, Brie and tomato quiche *13*, 204, *205*
asparagus, aubergine, Brie and tomato tortilla 204
asparagus, lemon and herb-stuffed salmon *13*, 148, *149*
crispy prosciutto and chargrilled asparagus salad 42
grilled lemon salmon with asparagus 148
lemony salmon and asparagus 148
prosciutto and asparagus pizza 42
prosciutto and asparagus tart *14*, 42, *43*

aubergines
asparagus, aubergine, Brie and tomato quiche *13*, 204, *205*
asparagus, aubergine, Brie and tomato tortilla 204
aubergine, Brie and tomato melted stacks 204
chicken in cheesy aubergine and tomato sauce 80
chicken Parmigiana *14*, 80, *81*
harissa aubergine and chickpea dip with flatbread crisps 220
harissa aubergine and hummus flatbreads 220, *221*

bacon
bacon, pine nut and parsnip gratin 48
bacon, pine nut and parsnip rosti 48
caramelized bacon and pine nut parsnips 48, *49*
creamy baked scallops and bacon 168
griddled scallops in bacon 168
scallop, bacon and pine nut pan-fry 168, *169*
bananas
banana and blueberry custard tarts 250
blueberry and banana French toast *18*, 250, *251*
blueberry pancakes with banana 250
brioche, banana and maple syrup pudding 274
brioche toasts with banana and maple syrup 274
pan-fried banana and maple syrup brioche rolls *19*, 274, *275*
beans
Cajun prawn rice and peas 150
Caribbean chicken, rice and pea pot 92
Caribbean chicken with rice and peas *15*, 92, *93*
chunky sausage and bean soup 24
easy cassoulet *12*, 24, *25*
garlicky pork and butter bean stew 36
garlicky pork with warm butter bean salad *18*, 36, *37*
griddled lamb cutlets and tomatoes with bean mash 44, *45*
lamb, tomato and bean pan-fry 44
pork with garlicky butter bean mash 36

prawn jambalaya *15*, 150, *151*
roast lamb with beans and tomatoes 44
smoky sausage and beans on toast 24
spicy sausage, rosemary and bean hot pot *18*, 62, *63*
spicy sausage, rosemary and bean pan-fry 62
tomato and bean soup 198
tuna and bean pasta salad *16*, 132, *133*
tuna and bean pitta pockets 132
beef
beef, pumpkin and prune soup 64
beef, pumpkin and prune stew *18*, 64, *65*
blackberry and red cabbage stew 68
creamy peppered steaks with sweet potato chips *19*, 38, *39*
fillet steaks with easy braised red cabbage and blackberries *13*, 68, *69*
peppered steak wraps 38
speedy beef, tomato and prune pan-fry 64
spiced beef and onion chapattis *15*, 52, *53*
spiced beef and onion curry 52
spicy beef rolls with onions 52
steaks with blackberry sauce and red cabbage 68
beetroot
carrot and beetroot couscous 222
carrot, beetroot and feta gratin 222
chickpea burgers with beetroot 186
falafels with beetroot salad and mint yoghurt *17*, 186, *187*
roasted carrot and beetroot pearl barley with feta *16*, 222, *223*
berries
apple and blackberry compote with almond scones 266, *267*
banana and blueberry custard tarts 250
berry and white chocolate tarts 246, *247*
blackberry and red cabbage stew 68
blueberry and banana French toast *18*, 250, *251*
blueberry pancakes with banana 250
caramelized berry rice pudding 240, *241*
caramelized rice pudding with warm berries 240

fillet steaks with easy braised red cabbage and blackberries *13*, 68, *69*

iced berries with hot white chocolate sauce 246

rice pudding berry meringues 240

steaks with blackberry sauce and red cabbage 68

white chocolate and blackberry turnovers 246

broccoli

teriyaki salmon with sesame broccoli 142

bulgar wheat

chicken and Med veg kebabs with herby bulgar wheat 108

warm chicken, Med veg and bulgar wheat salad *17*, 108, *109*

butternut squash

butternut soup with antipasti peppers 194

creamy squash, pine nuts and stuffed pasta 192

goats' cheese and butternut squash stuffed peppers 212, *213*

red pepper, butternut and goats' cheese soup 212

roasted butternut and red pepper soup 194

roasted chicken and spiced butternut squash *19*, 112, *113*

spiced butternut squash soup *15*, 194, *195*

spiced chicken and butternut soup 112

stuffed pasta, pine nut and butternut gratin *17*, 192, *193*

cabbage

blackberry and red cabbage stew 68

fillet steaks with easy braised red cabbage and blackberries *13*, 68, *69*

steaks with blackberry sauce and red cabbage 68

carrots

carrot and beetroot couscous 222

carrot, beetroot and feta gratin 222

pan-fried chicken, carrots and thyme 102

quick Thai crab cakes with carrot salad 144

roasted carrot and beetroot pearl barley with feta *16*, 222, *223*

sticky chicken with carrots and thyme 102

Thai crab cakes with carrot noodle salad *15*, 144, *145*

Thai crab and carrot salad 144

thyme-roasted chicken and carrots *12*, 102, *103*

cauliflower

curried cauliflower, lentil and rice pot *15*, 184, *185*

easy cauliflower and lentil pilau 184

speedy cauliflower pilau 184

cheese

asparagus, aubergine, Brie and tomato quiche *13*, 204, *205*

asparagus, aubergine, Brie and tomato tortilla 204

aubergine, Brie and tomato melted stacks 204

baked herby cod with Gruyère and spinach mash *18*, 158, *159*

blue cheese, spinach and walnut gnocchi bake 208

blue cheese, spinach and walnut tart 208

carrot, beetroot and feta gratin 222

cheat's chicken parmigiana 80

cheesy courgette bakes *17*, 188, *189*

cheesy courgette carbonara 188

cheesy pea and mint rice balls 210

chicken and dolcelatte pasta bake *13*, 78, *79*

chicken and dolcelatte pasta gratin 78

chicken and dolcelatte tagliatelle 78

chicken Parmigiana *14*, 80, *81*

courgette and Cheddar omelette 188

creamy chicken, gammon and leek gratin 122

creamy salmon with herbs 156

creamy salmon pie with herby mash 156

fully loaded chicken nachos 94

garlic and herb Brie stuffed mushrooms 196

garlic and herb mushroom tart *196*, 196

goats' cheese and butternut squash stuffed peppers 212, *213*

herby cod with cheesy spinach and mash pots 158

herby mozzarella and tomato naan pizza 226

lamb burgers with herb and feta couscous 30

lamb meatballs with herby feta couscous *14*, 30, *31*

leek-stuffed chicken in prosciutto 122

mozzarella, tomato and basil salad with dough balls 226

mozzarella, tomato and basil thin-crust pizza 226, *227*

pan-fried cod with herby cheese mash 158

pan-fried herby salmon with creamy mascarpone sauce *12*, 156, *157*

paprika chicken quesadillas *15*, 88, *89*

pea, feta and mint pilaf 210

pea, leek and potato soup with pesto and cheesy toasts *12*, 182, *183*

pea, Parmesan and mint risotto 210, *211*

pepper, caper and spinach penne bake 218

pepperoni, artichoke and olive pizzas 34, *35*

pesto fish pie 130

quick hot-smoked haddock rarebits 140

red pepper, butternut and goats' cheese soup 212

red pepper and goats' cheese bruschetta 212

roasted carrot and beetroot pearl barley with feta 222, *223*

simple spinach and feta wraps 206

smoked fish and fennel crêpes 152

smoked haddock rarebit 140, *141*

smoked haddock rarebit tart 140

spicy sweetcorn fondue 190

spinach and feta burritos 206

spinach and feta filo parcels *14*, 180, *181*

spinach and feta salad tarts 180

spinach and feta tortilla pies 180

spinach tortellini, walnut and blue cheese gratin 208, *209*

tomato and mozzarella sourdough bake 200

tomato and mozzarella sourdough bruschetta *14*, 200, *201*

warm spinach and feta tortilla slices *206*, 206

warm tomato and mozzarella salad with sourdough croûtons 200

chicken
baked chicken with creamy tarragon sauce 98
baked lemon and parsley chicken 96
Caribbean chicken, rice and pea pot 92
Caribbean chicken with rice and peas 15, 92, 93
cheat's chicken parmigiana 80
chicken, artichoke and olive pan-fry 100
chicken, artichoke and olive pasta 100
chicken in cheesy aubergine and tomato sauce 80
chicken and chorizo with green lentils 104, 105
chicken and chorizo kebabs with lentil purée 104
chicken and dolcelatte pasta bake 13, 78, 79
chicken and dolcelatte pasta gratin 78
chicken and dolcelatte tagliatelle 78
chicken jalfrezi 15, 118, 119
chicken and Med veg kebabs with herby bulgar wheat 108
chicken, pancetta and mushroom carbonara 19, 106, 107
chicken, pancetta and mushroom pasta bake 106
chicken Parmigiana 14, 80, 81
chicken, potato and pea curry 76
chicken, potato and spinach pan-fry 17, 110, 111
chicken saag aloo 76
chicken, spinach and potato gratin 110
chicken and sweet potato curry 76, 77
chicken and sweetcorn chowder 12, 86, 87
chicken tortilla toasties 88
creamy chicken, gammon and leek gratin 122
creamy chicken, gammon and leek pan-fry 12, 122, 123
creamy chicken, pancetta and mushroom pasta 106
creamy chicken and sweetcorn chowder 86
creamy chicken and tarragon pan-fry 98

creamy chicken and tarragon pasta 18, 98, 99
easy cassoulet 24, 25
fully loaded chicken nachos 94
Greek chicken stifado 14, 100, 101
honeyed chicken and roasted rosemary roots 18, 120, 121
leek-stuffed chicken in prosciutto 122
lemon chicken and courgette risotto 82
lemon chicken and courgette stir-fry 82
lemon and parsley chicken skewers 16, 96, 97
lemon and parsley-stuffed chicken 96
Mexican chicken burgers with tomato salad 16, 94, 95
Mexican roasted chicken tortillas 94
Oriental chicken satay stir-fry 15, 114, 115
pan-fried chicken, carrots and thyme 102
paprika chicken quesadillas 15, 88, 89
quick Caribbean chicken 92
quick chicken satay stir-fry 114
quick chicken and sweetcorn soup 86
roasted chicken and spiced butternut squash 19, 112, 113
roasted lemony chicken with courgettes 82, 83
rosemary and honey-glazed chicken and roots 120
satay chicken skewers with Oriental veg stir-fry 114
simple chicken and spinach with mash 110
simple honeyed rosemary chicken and roots 120
smoky chicken quesadillas with sweetcorn salsa 88
speedy chicken curry 118
spiced chicken and butternut soup 112
spiced chicken and plantain stew 116
spicy chicken and plantain with Caribbean sauce 15, 116, 117
spicy chicken with soy and pineapple noodles 90
spicy chicken stir-fry 118

spicy chicken strips with sweet potatoes 112
sticky chicken with carrots and thyme 102
sticky soy chicken with fruity Oriental salad 17, 90, 91
sticky soy chicken and pineapple skewers 90
Thai chicken and veg kebab wraps 16, 84, 85
Thai chicken and veg noodles 84
Thai chicken with veg rice 84
thyme-roasted chicken and carrots 12, 102, 103
warm chicken, Med veg and bulgar wheat salad 17, 108, 109
warm chicken and Med veg pittas 108

chickpeas
chickpea, artichoke and tomato pan-fry 17, 202, 203
chickpea burgers with beetroot 186
falafels with beetroot salad and mint yoghurt 17, 186, 187
harissa aubergine and chickpea dip with flatbread crisps 220
harissa aubergine and chickpea flatbreads 220
harissa lamb and chickpeas 50
harissa lamb pittas with hummus 50
Moroccan lamb kebabs with warm chickpea salad 15, 50, 51
one-pan harissa lamb and chickpeas 50
rustic chickpea and tomato dip 202
speedy chickpea dahl 216
warm chickpea, artichoke and tomato stew 202

chocolate
baked chocolate orange mousse 13, 278, 279
berry and white chocolate tarts 246, 247
chilled chocolate and orange mousse 278
chocolate dipped fruits 256
chocolate honeycomb crunch 256
chocolate melting middle puddings 19, 244, 245
chocolate sponge and custard 244
chocolate tiffin squares 18, 256, 257
iced berries with hot white chocolate sauce 246

speedy chocolate orange creams 278

warm chocolate croissant pudding 244

white chocolate and blackberry turnovers 246

chorizo
baked eggs with chorizo and ham 70

chicken and chorizo with green lentils 104, 105

chicken and chorizo kebabs with lentil purée 104

chorizo and ham eggs 12, 70, 71

chorizo and ham tortilla 70

chorizo-topped lamb with spicy chips 40

lamb and chorizo burgers with roasted new potatoes 18, 40, 41

quick lamb burgers with chorizo 40

cod
baked herby cod with Gruyère and spinach mash 18, 158, 159

chilli and lemon fishcakes 17, 164, 165

cod rolls with tartare sauce 170

crispy pesto baked cod 12, 130, 131

deep-fried chilli cod balls 164

herby cod with cheesy spinach and mash pots 158

juicy cod burgers with tartare sauce 19, 170, 171

pan-fried cod with herby cheese mash 158

pesto fish pie 130

coffee
cappuccino fudge creams 234

speedy iced tiramisu 14, 234

tiramisu 234

courgettes
cheesy courgette bakes 17, 188, 189

cheesy courgette carbonara 188

courgette and Cheddar omelette 188

lemon chicken and courgette risotto 82

lemon chicken and courgette stir-fry 82

roasted lemony chicken with courgettes 82, 83

couscous
carrot and beetroot couscous 222

lamb burgers with herb and feta couscous 30

lamb meatballs with herby feta couscous 14, 30, 31

Moroccan lamb meatballs with herby couscous 30

pan-fried ginger and lime mackerel with roasted veg couscous 136

stir-fried balsamic lamb with couscous 26

crab
gingered prawn and crab rice 172

Oriental prawn and crab stir-fry 16, 172, 173

prawn and crab spring rolls 172

quick Thai crab cakes with carrot salad 144

Thai crab cakes with carrot noodle salad 144, 145

Thai crab and carrot salad 144

dates
orange and pistachio polenta muffins with dates 272, 273

simple date and pistachio oranges 272

eggs
asparagus, aubergine, Brie and tomato tortilla 204

baked eggs with chorizo and ham 70

baked spinach and leek frittata 224

chorizo and ham eggs 12, 70, 71

chorizo and ham tortilla 70

courgette and Cheddar omelette 188

eggs Benedict 19, 32, 33

leek and spinach omelette 224

Niçoise pasta salad 132

pan-cooked eggs with spinach and leeks 224

poached eggs on ham rosti cakes 32

falafel and beetroot pizzas 186

falafels with beetroot salad and mint yoghurt 17, 186, 187

fennel
ginger and lime mackerel with fennel salad and new potatoes 136

ginger and lime mackerel with roasted veg 16, 136, 137

Greek chicken stifado 14, 100, 101

pan-fried herb and garlic sea bass and fennel 166

roasted garlicky herb sea bass, fennel and potatoes 19, 166, 167

smoked fish and fennel crêpes 152

smoked fish and fennel pan-fry 152

smoked fish and fennel pie 17, 152, 153

figs
baked honeyed figs and raspberries 16, 232, 233

fig, raspberry and honey brûlées 232

fig, raspberry and honey yoghurt pots 232

fish
fish finger baguettes with pesto mayo 130

fish finger rolls with tartare sauce 170

smoked fish and fennel pie 17, 152, 153

Thai green fish curry with lime leaves 16, 160, 161

fishcakes
chilli and lemon fishcakes 17, 164, 165

Thai-style fishcakes 160

fruit
cheat's fruit compote cobbler 266

chocolate dipped fruits 256

filo fruit pies with pistachio yoghurt 254

fruit compote with drop scones 266

grilled fruit parcels with pistachio yoghurt 14, 254, 255

pan-fried Marsala fruit and almonds 276

tropical fruit and coconut cheesecakes 258, 259

tropical fruit salad with coconut cream 258

warm fruit and pistachio compote 254

ham
baked eggs with chorizo and ham 70

chicken livers in prosciutto with walnut salad 58

chorizo and ham eggs 12, 70, 71

chorizo and ham tortilla 70

creamy chicken, gammon and leek gratin 122

creamy chicken, gammon and leek pan-fry 12, 122, 123

crispy prosciutto and chargrilled asparagus salad 42

eggs Benedict *19*, 32, *33*
grilled salmon with creamy prosciutto sauce 174
leek-stuffed chicken in prosciutto 122
pan-fried prosciutto-wrapped salmon *19*, 174, *175*
poached eggs on ham rosti cakes 32
prosciutto and asparagus pizza 42
prosciutto and asparagus tart *14*, 42, *43*
prosciutto, chicken liver and walnut ragù 58
roasted prosciutto-wrapped salmon and potatoes 174
warm prosciutto, chicken liver and walnut salad *17*, 58, *59*

lamb
balsamic lamb with rosemary rosties 26
balsamic lamb steaks with parsnip and potato mash *13*, 26, *27*
griddled lamb cutlets and tomatoes with bean mash 44, *45*
harissa lamb and chickpeas 50
harissa lamb pittas with hummus 50
lamb burgers with herb and feta couscous 30
lamb and chorizo burgers with roasted new potatoes *18*, 40, *41*
lamb meatballs with herby feta couscous *14*, 30, *31*
lamb, tomato and bean pan-fry 44
lamb and vegetable pilaf 66
lamb and vegetable risotto 66
Moroccan lamb kebabs with warm chickpea salad *15*, 50, *51*
Moroccan lamb meatballs with herby couscous 30
one-pan harissa lamb and chickpeas 50
quick lamb burgers with chorizo 40
risotto-topped lamb and vegetable pie *14*, 66, *67*
roast lamb with beans and tomatoes 44
stir-fried balsamic lamb with couscous 26
leeks
baked spinach and leek frittata 224
chunky pea, leek and pesto soup 182
creamy chicken, gammon and leek gratin 122

creamy chicken, gammon and leek pan-fry *12*, 122, *123*
leek and spinach omelette 224
leek-stuffed chicken in prosciutto 122
pan-cooked eggs with spinach and leeks 224
pea, leek and potato soup with pesto and cheesy toasts *12*, 182, *183*
lemons
asparagus, lemon and herb-stuffed salmon *13*, 148, *149*
baked lemon and parsley chicken 96
chilli and lemon tuna balls 164
grilled lemon salmon with asparagus 148
lemon Eton mess with strawberries 248
lemon Madeira and strawberry trifle 248
lemon and parsley chicken skewers *16*, 96, *97*
lemon and parsley-stuffed chicken 96
lemon and passionfruit syllabubs 264
lemon and passionfruit whips 264, *265*
lemon polenta cake with vanilla strawberries 248, *249*
lemony salmon and asparagus 148
saucy lemon and passionfruit pudding 264
lentils
chicken and chorizo with green lentils 104, 105
curried cauliflower, lentil and rice pot *15*, 184, *185*
easy cauliflower and lentil pilau 184
red lentil dhal with warm naan 216
yellow lentil dahl 216
liver
chicken livers in prosciutto with walnut salad 58
pan-fried liver with caper sauce and root mash *17*, 60, *61*
pan-fried liver and capers with sautéed parsnips 60
prosciutto, chicken liver and walnut ragù 58
quick liver and capers 60
warm prosciutto, chicken liver and walnut salad *17*, 58, *59*

mackerel
ginger and lime mackerel with fennel salad and new potatoes 136
ginger and lime mackerel with roasted veg *16*, 136, *137*
pan-fried ginger and lime mackerel with roasted veg couscous 136
mangoes
coconut, mango and lime layers 258
mushrooms
chicken, pancetta and mushroom carbonara *19*, 106, *107*
chicken, pancetta and mushroom pasta bake 106
creamy chicken, pancetta and mushroom pasta 106
garlic and herb Brie stuffed mushrooms 196
garlic and herb mushroom tart *196*, 196
garlic and herb mushrooms with potato cakes 196
peppered steak stroganoff 38
mussels
chilli seafood stew *15*, 162, *163*
garlicky cider mussels with chips 128
mussel, garlic and cider tagliatelle 128
mussels with cider and garlic sauce *13*, 128, *129*
spicy seafood soup 162

nectarines
baked almond peaches and nectarines 276
noodles
spicy chicken with soy and pineapple noodles 90
sweet chilli and tempura vegetable noodles 214
teriyaki salmon with egg noodles *16*, 142, *143*
teriyaki salmon stir-fry 142
Thai chicken and veg noodles 84
Thai crab cakes with carrot noodle salad *15*, 144, *145*
Thai crab and carrot salad 144
nuts
apple and blackberry compote with almond scones 266, *267*
bacon, pine nut and parsnip gratin 48
bacon, pine nut and parsnip rosti 48

blue cheese, spinach and walnut gnocchi bake 208

blue cheese, spinach and walnut tart 208

caramelized bacon and pine nut parsnips 48, *49*

chicken livers in prosciutto with walnut salad 58

creamy pumpkin and pine nut stuffed pasta 192

creamy squash, pine nuts and stuffed pasta 192

prosciutto, chicken liver and walnut ragù 58

scallop, bacon and pine nut pan-fry 168, *169*

spinach tortellini, walnut and blue cheese gratin 208, *209*

stuffed pasta, pine nut and butternut gratin *17*, 192, *193*

warm prosciutto, chicken liver and walnut salad *17*, 58, *59*

olives

chicken, artichoke and olive pan-fry 100

chicken, artichoke and olive pasta 100

crispy pesto baked cod 130, *131*

Greek chicken stifado *14*, 100, *101*

pepperoni, artichoke and olive crostini 34

pepperoni, artichoke and olive pizzas *14*, 34, *35*

pepperoni, artichoke and olive tart 34

onions

spiced beef and onion chapattis *15*, 52, *53*

spiced beef and onion curry 52

spicy beef rolls with onions 52

oranges

baked chocolate orange mousse *13*, 278, *279*

caramelized marmalade oranges 262

chilled chocolate and orange mousse 278

orange and pistachio polenta muffins with dates 272, *273*

orange polenta pancakes with dates and pistachios 272

plum and orange fool 236

roasted plum and orange compote with granola *16*, 236, *237*

simple date and pistachio oranges 272

simple pan-fried orangey plums 236

sticky marmalade microwave puds 262

sticky soy chicken with fruity Oriental salad *17*, 90

warm marmalade puddings 262, *263*

Oriental prawn and crab stir-fry *16*, 172, *173*

pancetta

chicken, pancetta and mushroom carbonara *19*, 106, *107*

chicken, pancetta and mushroom pasta bake 106

creamy chicken, pancetta and mushroom pasta 106

parsnips

bacon, pine nut and parsnip gratin 48

bacon, pine nut and parsnip rosti 48

balsamic lamb with rosemary rosties 26

balsamic lamb steaks with parsnip and potato mash *13*, 26, *27*

caramelized bacon and pine nut parsnips 48, *49*

pan-fried liver and capers with sautéed parsnips 60

passionfruit

lemon and passionfruit syllabubs 264

lemon and passionfruit whips 264, *265*

saucy lemon and passionfruit pudding 264

pasta

antipasti pepper, caper and spinach pasta 218

baked anchovy tomatoes with spaghetti 138, *139*

cheesy courgette carbonara 188

chicken and dolcelatte pasta bake *13*, 78, *79*

chicken and dolcelatte pasta gratin 78

chicken and dolcelatte tagliatelle 78

chicken, pancetta and mushroom carbonara *19*, 106, *107*

chicken, pancetta and mushroom pasta bake 106

creamy chicken, pancetta and mushroom pasta 106

creamy chicken and tarragon pasta *18*, 98, *99*

creamy seafood pasta 146

mussel, garlic and cider tagliatelle 128

Niçoise pasta salad 132

pepper, caper and spinach pappardelle gratins 218, *219*

pepper, caper and spinach penne bake 218

seafood tagliatelle *13*, 146, *147*

spaghetti puttanesca 138

spicy sausage pasta bake 28

spicy sausages and rocket baguettes 28

spicy sausage and rocket pasta *28*, 28, *29*

stuffed pasta, pine nut and butternut gratin *17*, 192, *193*

tuna and bean pasta salad *16*, 132, *133*

peaches

apple and peach marzipan crumble 270

apple and peach marzipan slice *19*, 270, *271*

baked almond peaches and nectarines 276

grilled marzipan peaches 270

pan-fried peach and plum cinnamon crunch *18*, 268, *269*

peach and plum clafoutis 268

peach and plum pancakes 268

peas

cheesy pea and mint rice balls 210

chicken, potato and pea curry 76

chunky pea, leek and pesto soup 182

pea, feta and mint pilaf 210

pea, leek and potato soup with pesto and cheesy toasts *12*, 182, *183*

pea, Parmesan and mint risotto 210, *211*

pea and pesto soup 182

speedy cauliflower pilau 184

pepperoni

pepperoni, artichoke and olive crostini 34

pepperoni, artichoke and olive pizzas *14*, 34, *35*

pepperoni, artichoke and olive tart 34

peppers

antipasti pepper, caper and spinach pasta 218

butternut soup with antipasti peppers 194

chicken jalfrezi *15*, 118, *119*
goats' cheese and butternut squash
    stuffed peppers 212, *213*
Oriental chicken satay stir-fry *15*,
    114, *115*
pepper, caper and spinach
    pappardelle gratins 218, *219*
pepper, caper and spinach penne
    bake 218
pork, sweetcorn and red pepper
    stir-fry 46
prawn jambalaya *15*, 150, *151*
red pepper, butternut and goats'
    cheese soup 212
red pepper and goats' cheese
    bruschetta 212
red pepper pork with creamed corn
    46
roasted butternut and red pepper
    soup 194
Tex-Mex pork ribs with sweetcorn
    and red pepper salsa 46, *47*
pineapple
    pineapple fritters with rum sauce
        252
    spiced pan-fried pineapple with rum
        252, *253*
    spicy chicken with soy and pineapple
        noodles 90
    sticky soy chicken and pineapple
        skewers 90
    upside-down pineapple and rum tart
        252
plantains
    spiced chicken and plantain stew
        116
    spicy chicken and plantain with
        Caribbean sauce *15*, 116, *117*
    spicy chicken with plantain chips
        116
plums
    pan-fried peach and plum cinnamon
        crunch *18*, 268, *269*
    peach and plum clafoutis 268
    peach and plum pancakes 268
    plum and orange fool 236
    roasted plum and orange compote
        with granola *16*, 236, *237*
    simple pan-fried orangey plums 236
pork
    creamy pork, apple and mustard
        pan-fry *12*, 54, *55*
    garlicky pork and butter bean stew
        36

garlicky pork with warm butter bean
    salad *18*, 36, *37*
pork, apple and mustard gratins 54
pork with garlicky butter bean mash
    36
pork, sweetcorn and red pepper
    stir-fry 46
red pepper pork with creamed corn
    46
simple pork, apple and mustard
    pan-fry 54
Tex-Mex pork ribs with sweetcorn
    and red pepper salsa 46, *47*
potatoes
    baked herby cod with Gruyère and
        spinach mash *18*, 158, *159*
    balsamic lamb with rosemary rosties
        26
    balsamic lamb steaks with parsnip
        and potato mash *13*, 26, *27*
    chicken, potato and pea curry 76
    chicken, potato and spinach pan-fry
        17, 110, 111
    chicken, spinach and potato gratin
        110
    chilli and lemon fishcakes *17*, 164,
        165
    creamy salmon pie with herby mash
        156
    deep-fried chilli cod balls 164
    garlicky cider mussels with chips
        128
    ginger and lime mackerel with
        roasted veg *16*, 136, *137*
    herby cod with cheesy spinach and
        mash pots 158
    lamb and chorizo burgers with
        roasted new potatoes *18*, 40, *41*
    pan-fried cod with herby cheese
        mash 158
    pea, leek and potato soup with pesto
        and cheesy toasts *12*, 182, *183*
    poached eggs on ham rosti cakes 32
    roasted garlicky herb sea bass, fennel
        and potatoes *19*, 166, *167*
    roasted prosciutto-wrapped salmon
        and potatoes 174
    salt, pepper and chilli squid with
        chips and garlic mayo *14*, 134,
        135
    sausages in red wine with creamy
        layered potatoes *19*, 56, *57*
    sausages in red wine gravy with
        cheesy potatoes 56

simple chicken and spinach with
    mash 110
sweetcorn rosti with chilli salsa 190
prawns
    Cajun prawn rice and peas 150
    Cajun-spiced prawns 150
    chilled coconut soup with sizzling
        prawns 154, *155*
    creamy salmon pie with herby mash
        156
    gingered prawn and crab rice 172
    Oriental prawn and crab stir-fry *16*,
        172, *173*
    prawn and coconut curry 154
    prawn and coconut pan-fry 154
    prawn and crab spring rolls 172
    prawn jambalaya *15*, 150, *151*
    Thai green fish curry with lime leaves
        16, 160, *161*
    Thai prawn stir-fry 160
prunes
    beef, pumpkin and prune soup 64
    beef, pumpkin and prune stew *18*,
        64, *65*
    speedy beef, tomato and prune
        pan-fry 64
pumpkin
    beef, pumpkin and prune soup 64
    beef, pumpkin and prune stew *18*,
        64, *65*
    creamy pumpkin and pine nut stuffed
        pasta 192

raspberries
    baked honeyed figs and raspberries
        16, 232, *233*
    fig, raspberry and honey brûlées
        232
    fig, raspberry and honey yoghurt
        pots 232
    floating islands with raspberries 260
    mini baked Alaskas 260
    soft raspberry meringues 260, *261*
rice
    Cajun prawn rice and peas 150
    caramelized berry rice pudding 240,
        241
    caramelized rice pudding with warm
        berries 240
    Caribbean chicken, rice and pea pot
        92
    Caribbean chicken with rice and peas
        15, 92, *93*
    cheesy pea and mint rice balls 210

curried cauliflower, lentil and rice pot 15, 184, 185
gingered prawn and crab rice 172
lamb and vegetable pilaf 66
lamb and vegetable risotto 66
lemon chicken and courgette risotto 82
pea, feta and mint pilaf 210
pea, Parmesan and mint risotto 210, 211
prawn jambalaya 15, 150, 151
rice pudding berry meringues 240
risotto-topped lamb and vegetable pie 14, 66, 67
simple seafood risotto 146
speedy cauliflower pilau 184
Thai chicken with veg rice 84
rocket
  spicy sausage and rocket baguettes 28
  spicy sausage and rocket pasta 18, 28, 29

salmon
  asparagus, lemon and herb-stuffed salmon 13, 148, 149
  creamy salmon with herbs 156
  creamy salmon pie with herby mash 156
  grilled lemon salmon with asparagus 148
  grilled salmon with creamy prosciutto sauce 174
  lemony salmon and asparagus 148
  pan-fried herby salmon with creamy mascarpone sauce 12, 156, 157
  pan-fried prosciutto-wrapped salmon 19, 174, 175
  roasted prosciutto-wrapped salmon and potatoes 174
  teriyaki salmon with egg noodles 16, 142, 143
  teriyaki salmon with sesame broccoli 142
  teriyaki salmon stir-fry 142
sausages
  chunky sausage and bean soup 24
  easy cassoulet 12, 24, 25
  sausage ball and red wine pan-fry 56
  sausages in red wine with creamy layered potatoes 19, 56, 57
  sausages in red wine gravy with cheesy potatoes 56

smoky sausage and beans on toast 24
spicy sausage pasta bake 28
spicy sausage and rocket baguettes 28
spicy sausage, rosemary and bean hot pot 18, 62, 63
spicy sausage, rosemary and bean pan-fry 62
spicy sausage and rosemary sandwiches 62
spicy sausages and rocket pasta 18, 28, 29
scallops
  creamy baked scallops and bacon 168
  griddled scallops in bacon 168
  scallop, bacon and pine nut pan-fry 168, 169
sea bass
  pan-fried herb and garlic sea bass and fennel 166
  roasted garlicky herb sea bass, fennel and potatoes 19, 166, 167
  sea bass fillets with garlic and herb butter 166
seafood
  chilli seafood stew 15, 162, 163
  creamy seafood pasta 146
  seafood, chilli and tomato pan-fry 162
  seafood tagliatelle 13, 146, 147
  simple seafood risotto 146
  spicy seafood soup 162
smoked haddock
  quick hot-smoked haddock rarebits 140
  smoked fish and fennel crêpes 152
  smoked fish and fennel pan-fry 152
  smoked fish and fennel pie 17, 152, 153
  smoked haddock rarebit 140, 141
  smoked haddock rarebit tart 140
spinach
  antipasti pepper, caper and spinach pasta 218
  baked herby cod with Gruyère and spinach mash 18, 158, 159
  baked spinach and leek frittata 224
  blue cheese, spinach and walnut gnocchi bake 208
  chicken, potato and spinach pan-fry 17, 110, 111
  chicken, spinach and potato gratin 110

herby cod with cheesy spinach and mash pots 158
leek and spinach omelette 224
pan-cooked eggs with spinach and leeks 224
pepper, caper and spinach pappardelle gratins 218, 219
pepper, caper and spinach penne bake 218
simple chicken and spinach with mash 110
simple spinach and feta wraps 206
smoked haddock rarebit 140, 141
spinach and feta burritos 206
spinach and feta filo parcels 14, 180, 181
spinach and feta salad tarts 180
spinach and feta tortilla pies 180
spinach tortellini, walnut and blue cheese gratin 208, 209
warm spinach and feta tortilla slices 206, 206
squid
  chilli seafood stew 15, 162, 163
  crispy squid with chilli dipping sauce 134
  polenta chilli squid with lime mayo 134
  salt, pepper and chilli squid with chips and garlic mayo 134, 135
  spicy seafood soup 162
strawberries
  crushed strawberry and lime shortbreads 238
  lemon Eton mess with strawberries 248
  lemon Madeira and strawberry trifle 248
  lemon polenta cake with vanilla strawberries 248, 249
  strawberry and lime biscuit stacks 238
  strawberry and lime brandy snap baskets 238
sweet potatoes
  chicken and sweet potato curry 76, 77
  creamy peppered steaks with sweet potato chips 19, 38, 39
  spicy chicken strips with sweet potatoes 112
sweetcorn
  Caribbean chicken, rice and pea pot 92

Caribbean chicken with rice and peas 15, 92, 93
chicken and sweetcorn chowder 12, 86, 87
creamy chicken and sweetcorn chowder 86
pork, sweetcorn and red pepper stir-fry 46
quick chicken and sweetcorn soup 86
red pepper pork with creamed corn 46
smoky chicken quesadillas with sweetcorn salsa 88
spicy sweetcorn fondue 190
sweetcorn fritters with sweet chilli dip 190, 191
sweetcorn rosti with chilli salsa 190
Tex-Mex pork ribs with sweetcorn and red pepper salsa 46, 47

tomatoes
anchovy tomato toasts 138
asparagus, aubergine, Brie and tomato quiche 13, 204, 205
asparagus, aubergine, Brie and tomato tortilla 204
aubergine, Brie and tomato melted stacks 204
baked anchovy tomatoes with spaghetti 138, 139
chicken in cheesy aubergine and tomato sauce 80
chicken Parmigiana 14, 80, 81
chickpea, artichoke and tomato pan-fry 17, 202, 203
crispy pesto baked cod 12, 130, 131
easy tomato and basil soup 198
ginger and lime mackerel with roasted veg 16, 136, 137
griddled lamb cutlets and tomatoes with bean mash 44, 45

herby mozzarella and tomato naan pizza 226
lamb, tomato and bean pan-fry 44
Mediterranean tomato soup 14, 198, 199
Mexican chicken burgers with tomato salad 16, 94, 95
mozzarella, tomato and basil salad with dough balls 226
mozzarella, tomato and basil thin-crust pizza 226, 227
quick hot-smoked haddock rarebits 140
roast lamb with beans and tomatoes 44
rustic chickpea and tomato dip 202
seafood, chilli and tomato pan-fry 162
smoked haddock rarebit 140, 141
spaghetti puttanesca 138
speedy beef, tomato and prune pan-fry 64
tomato and bean soup 198
tomato and mozzarella sourdough bake 200
tomato and mozzarella sourdough bruschetta 14, 200, 201
warm chickpea, artichoke and tomato stew 202
warm tomato and mozzarella salad with sourdough croûtons 200
tuna
chilli and lemon tuna balls 164
Niçoise pasta salad 132
tuna and bean pasta salad 16, 132, 133
tuna and bean pitta pockets 132

vegetables
chicken and Med veg kebabs with herby bulgar wheat 108
ginger and lime mackerel with roasted veg 16, 136, 137

honeyed chicken and roasted rosemary roots 18, 120, 121
lamb and vegetable pilaf 66
lamb and vegetable risotto 66
Oriental prawn and crab stir-fry 16, 172, 173
pan-fried ginger and lime mackerel with roasted veg couscous 136
pan-fried liver with caper sauce and root mash 17, 60, 61
quick chicken satay stir-fry 114
risotto-topped lamb and vegetable pie 14, 66, 67
roasted lemony chicken with courgettes 82, 83
rosemary and honey-glazed chicken and roots 120
satay chicken skewers with Oriental veg stir-fry 114
simple honeyed rosemary chicken and roots 120
sweet chilli and tempura vegetable noodles 214
sweet chilli vegetable stir-fry 214
tempura mixed vegetables with chilli sauce 214
Thai chicken and veg kebab wraps 16, 84, 85
Thai chicken and veg noodles 84
Thai chicken with veg rice 84
warm chicken, Med veg and bulgar wheat salad 17, 108, 109
warm chicken and Med veg pittas 108

Acknowledgements

Recipes by: Emma Jane Frost and Nichola Palmer
Executive Editor: Eleanor Maxfield
Managing Editor: Clare Churly
Art Direction: Tracy Killick and Geoff Fennell for Tracy Killick Art Direction and Design
Original Design Concept: www.gradedesign.com
Designer: Tracy Killick Art Direction and Design
Photographer: Lis Parsons
Home Economist: Emma Jane Frost
Prop Stylist: Liz Hippisley
Senior Production Manager: Katherine Hockley